SINATRA

ALSO BY JOHN ROCKWELL

All American Music: Composition in the Late Twentieth Century

SINATRA

AN AMERICAN CLASSIC

JOHN ROCKWELL

Rolling Stone

A RANDOM HOUSE • ROLLING STONE PRESS BOOK

Design by Derek Ungless

Grateful acknowledgement is made to *The New York Times* for permission
to reprint from "The Bobby Sox Have Wilted, But the Memory Remains
Fresh," by Martha Weinman Lear, Arts and Leisure, October 13, 1974.

The Al Hirschfeld drawing of Frank Sinatra, page 95, is reproduced by
special arrangement with the Margo Feiden Galleries, New York.

All rights reserved under International and Pan-American Copyright
Conventions. Published in the United States by Random House, Inc., New
York, and simultaneously in Canada by Random House of Canada Limited,
Toronto.

Library of Congress Cataloging in Publication Data

Rockwell, John.
Sinatra: an American classic.

1. Sinatra, Frank, 1915–   . 2. Singers—
United States—Biography. I. Title.
ML420.S565R6 1984 784.5'0092'4 [B]   84–42738
ISBN 0-394-53977-X

Manufactured in the United States of America
10 9 8 7 6 5 4 3 2 1
First Edition

For Henry Pleasants and phrasing aficionados everywhere

獻給鄰居

ACKNOWLEDGMENTS

Thanks for advice and assistance to John S. Wilson, Stephen Holden, Robert Cornfield, Jann Wenner, Jonathan Wells, Erroll McDonald, Elisa Petrini, Derek Ungless, Ilene Cherna, Bob Merlis and Howard Thompson for "curvaceous"

The editors of Rolling Stone are grateful for the contributions of Karin Berg, Carrie Schneider, Mary Astadourian, Robert Coe, Janet Rab Ungless, Connie Scraft, Louise Marinis, Janice Borowicz, Frank Driggs, Louis and Carole Summa, Michael Ochs, and Neal Peters

SINATRA

RANK SINATRA is by any reasonable criterion the greatest singer in the history of American popular music and, by every measure, an extraordinarily complex man. His life has touched on innumerable facets of our culture over the past half-century—the struggle of ethnic subgroups within American society; the stylistic revolutions of popular music; the rise of electronic technology and its impact on the business of music; the connections between music and films, entertainment and the underworld, and entertainment and politics, left and right. His career has been shaped by the tangled links between classical music, jazz, pop and rock; by the ambivalent bonds between ethics and art; by the mass sexual hysteria of youth; by the pain of romantic love and the dry desperation of aging bachelorhood; by the personal distortions that celebrity status inflicts upon those who so eagerly desire to be celebrities, and succeed.

His is a remarkable story, and not surprisingly it has been told and retold. Curiously, however, and reflective of the interests of the popular American press, that story—even in the two largest books devoted to his life, those of Arnold

The very young Sinatra, in his first top hat and tails. He was raised in a working-class home, an only child in a neighborhood of large Catholic families.

Sinatra with his mother Natalie, nicknamed Dolly, on a country excursion in 1925.

Left: The Hoboken Four, with Sinatra at far right, on a 1935 nationwide tour sponsored by Major Bowes. Soon the young singer would leave the group to break into the radio circuit, attracting the attention of first Harry James and then Tommy Dorsey. Right: Sinatra with his mother and his fireman father, Martin. Even as a teenager, the kid from Hoboken exuded extraordinary self-confidence.

To Aunt Marge
— and Uncle Babe
Sincere regards and Best of luck
Frank Sinatra
"Frankie"

Shaw (*Sinatra: Twentieth-Century Romantic*, 1968) and Earl Wilson (*Sinatra*, 1976)—consists mostly of a tawdry procession of nightclub punch-outs and Mafia hearings. Everyone pays lip service to the idea that Sinatra is above all a singer, but then subverts that notion by concentrating on the obnoxious brawler and arrogant womanizer, the lowlife of the sleazy acquaintances and still sleazier press clippings. His biography certainly includes these tackier aspects. Perhaps he really has ties to the Mafia, as his detractors have insinuated for almost forty years. But nobody has laid a legal glove on him, and in the end his gangster image pales before his accomplishments as a musician, even as it augments his mysterious, extramusical aura. It is a cliché of Sinatra biography that his music ultimately excuses his life; perhaps, somehow, in the context of his personality and his times, each can explain the other.

Most Sinatra studies have been by men his own age. My perspective is from a different generation, one that came of age after the crucial watershed of the mid-Fifties, when rock & roll seemed to sweep aside all of Sinatra's values, musical and otherwise. If the time now seems right for a reconsideration of his achievement, it is only fitting that the recent exaltation of his reputation was at least partly inspired by rock & rollers.

Sid Vicious's hoarse and croaking rendition of "My Way," for instance, on the Sex Pistols' *Great Rock 'n' Roll Swindle* album of 1979, seemed at first to be merely another salvo in the eternal war between rude youth and middle-of-the-road schlock, a derisive dismissal of Sinatra and his anthem, the "Stairway to Heaven" of the geriatric generation. But like most of what the Sex Pistols did, this was no simple exercise in mockery. "My Way" was a French *chanson* before Paul Anka put American words to it; it became Sinatra's testimony through the sheer force of his interpretation and personality. Yet it fit Sid Vicious's life (and imminent death), too, as he knew. It is by no means hard to imagine that his version of Sinatra's most famous latter-day song was a not-so-secret tribute, an attestation of affinities between one of the fathers of punk rock and a man who, in his music, career and tempestuous character, became, in the words of the *Rolling Stone Encyclopedia of Rock & Roll*, "the model and envy of rockers from the beginning."

That might seem a strange fate for someone so closely identified with the prerock Tin Pan Alley tradition of American popular song. But Sinatra's style anticipated rock and folk-rock singing in surprising ways, above all in his insistence on conversational naturalness. More than that, he was one of the first mass-media youth idols, and managed to translate his early fame into a lasting recording and acting career still built upon a feisty, nose-thumbing defiance of society's sillier conventions.

With the covert tribute of their "My Way," as with so much else, the Sex Pistols led the pack. Sinatra's career has had its ups and downs, but recently there has been a remarkable surge of admiration for this self-described saloon singer, culminating in a string of achievements in late 1983 and early 1984. Rock, jazz and even classical critics have lavished on this seeming anachronism a respect bordering on—amounting to—veneration. The praise reached its peak with the release of a sixteen-disc audiophile boxed set of Sinatra's Capitol albums from the Fifties, notably in essays by the rock critic Stephen Holden for the *Atlantic* and the jazz critic Gary Giddins for *Stereo Review* when that magazine named Sinatra the winner of its 1984 Mabel Mercer award.

It wasn't just critics who shored up Sinatra's position in the pantheon; he was honored by the media, the arts establishment and his fellow artists. WNEW-AM in New York, which had reverted to its swing-era programming in 1979, grew fat and happy on a playlist that revolved devotionally around Sinatra's recordings. Joe Piscopo of the *Saturday Night Live* television show released a loving twelve-inch single called *I Love Rock 'n' Roll*, an eight-song rock medley sung with every Sinatra mannerism in the book.

In rock itself, the Pretenders played Sinatra's ebullient recording of "That's Life" to herald their arrival onstage during their 1984 United States tour. And Linda Ronstadt's album *What's New*, an overt emulation of Sinatra's classic collection of torch songs, *Only the Lonely*, with new accompaniments by Sinatra's favorite arranger, Nelson Riddle, shocked the record industry by going double platinum.

A Variety Clubs International Sinatra special included, amid the expected show-biz backslapping, some almost embarrassingly impassioned testimonials to Sinatra the musician and man from Richard Burton, Burt Reynolds and Carol Burnett. Twyla Tharp, the leading choreographer of her generation, made two separate, related ballets based on Sinatra's songs, both of them huge popular hits and one of them, the American Ballet Theater version with Mikhail Baryshnikov, seen on a December 1983 television special when Sinatra was named one of five winners of the annual honors for lifetime achievement in the arts at Kennedy Center in Washington.

This recognition comes on the eve of Sinatra's seventieth birthday and his fiftieth year as an entertainer, counting from his appearance with the Hoboken Four on the Major Bowes Amateur Hour in 1935. His commercially successful, constantly creative longevity is almost unprecedented. And at the end of that long span, Sinatra not only shows no signs of quitting but is singing with a technical assurance and, more crucially still, a personal conviction that put most performers, old and young, to shame.

Beyond the day-to-day details of his existence, his has been a life lived through song, and an honorable, demonstrably successful attempt to age gracefully as an American popular musician. He owes his strengths, and his limitations, to the clarity with which he spoke for his generation. But like any true artist, his impact transcends such parochialism, reaching out to speak of loves and fears common to us all. Frank Sinatra is preeminent among popular singers because his songs are, as Peter Bogdanovich once said, "not only his autobiography but ours as well."

FRANCIS ALBERT SINATRA was born in Hoboken, New Jersey, a working-class wharf town across the Hudson River from lower Manhattan, on December 12, 1915. Like so many performers who hope to appeal to young people, he cheated for a while on his birth year; during his youth-idol heyday, it was announced as 1917, but Sinatra eventually set that right when he started publicly celebrating his milestone birthdays. His father, Martin Sinatra, was a boilermaker and sometime boxer from Catania, on the east coast of Sicily, and his mother, Natalie, nicknamed Dolly, came from Genoa. His birthplace was an honorable working-class home—no slum disgrace, despite some later self-mythologizing—at 415 Monroe Street, a site that is now a dirt parking lot, distinguished only by a brick-and-wood arched gateway.

Sinatra's birth was a perilous one. The baby weighed thirteen and one half pounds, and the doctor damaged his left cheek and earlobe during the delivery—scars Sinatra never had masked by plastic surgery. At first the child appeared stillborn, so the doctor turned his attention to saving the mother. But Sinatra's

Left: The glee club was one of
Sinatra's principal interests at
Demarest High School before he
left in his sophomore year. After
he reached stardom, his press
agent had this early singing
experience re-created for the
cameras. Right: Being fitted for
his first tailor-made suit. Always
a dapper dresser, he acquired his
first nickname—Slacksey—
because he had more trousers
than anyone. His other moniker
was Angles, because he knew
them all.

Tommy Dorsey and his orchestra in *Las Vegas Nights* (1941), released in the heyday of the Hollywood formula musical. Sinatra, third from left, sang "I'll Never Smile Again"; *Down Beat* and *Metronome* would name him the best male band singer that year.

Above: During his time with
Dorsey, Sinatra often sang with
the band's harmony group, the
Pied Pipers. Here he commands
the mike with lead singer Jo
Stafford. Right: One of the top
bandleaders of the time, Dorsey
was a celebrated trombone player
whose smooth legato phrasing
would help shape Sinatra's
singing style.

maternal grandmother, Rosa Garavanti, who had nine children of her own, held the baby under a cold-water faucet until he sputtered to life.

He was an only child in a Catholic neighborhood marked by large families; some have speculated that his later entourage was born of this youthful loneliness. His early years were marked by a determined, and effective, desire to win friends through impulsive acts of generosity. He was popular at David E. Rue Junior High and Demarest High, if not especially devoted to his studies, and he was successful with girls, too, from an early age. Just as important for the formation of his character were a series of street encounters that hardened a pugnacious resolve that hasn't deserted him to this day. There were gangs on the waterfront, but it was the Depression fashion for film gangsters—models of macho bravado, antedating the rock & roll rebel—that shaped his self-image more decisively than subsequent acquaintanceship with real gangsters could ever do.

His parents had enough money to keep him in decent clothes—his nickname as a teenager was Slacksey O'Brien, which reflected in part his dapper attire and in part his father's fighting name of Marty O'Brien; the Irish, who had immigrated a few decades earlier, controlled the politics and constabulary of poor neighborhoods in those years, and the Italians were forced to accommodate themselves to Irish pols, judges and cops on every corner.

Dolly Sinatra was no docile housewife; she knew how to work within the prevailing power structures, familial and political. The young Sinatra was largely raised, at least at first, by Rosa Garavanti. His mother ascended rapidly in local Democratic politics—"a kind of Catherine de Medici of Hoboken's third ward," in Gay Talese's phrase, capable of delivering several hundred key votes and wielding tangible power within her sphere of influence. One beneficiary of that power was her husband, whom she made a fireman; he eventually rose to the rank of captain, some say again with her assistance.

Dolly helped her son's singing as well, although Sinatra showed plenty of signs of being able to advance his career all by himself. By his mid-teens, he knew what he wanted to do in life. This self-realization had been prompted by his attendance at concerts by Rudy Vallee and Bing Crosby, who became his idol. For a while Dolly Sinatra had more conventional ambitions for her only child— engineering, perhaps, or some form of business. "In your teens," he recalled later, "there's always someone to spit on your dreams."

But Dolly was soon converted by the intensity of her son's ambition, and not only abetted his fledgling singing career but grudgingly countenanced his dropping out of high school. By 1932 he had begun to make the rounds of local clubs, and his mother bought him a $65 portable sound system that he could carry with him on his dates and, perhaps, helped influence local club owners to engage her son. He, in turn, managed to finagle free sheet music from publishers, which enabled him to offer club owners not just his musical skills, such as they were, but money-saving amplification and band charts.

His stint with Major Bowes and his Amateur Hour organization in 1935 might have launched his big-time career, but it turned out instead to be only a hiatus in a seemingly endless round of obscure club dates. The Bowes operation consisted of regional and national auditions, with the finals broadcast live from New York and then nationwide tours for the winners. One way or another, Sinatra hooked up with three other young men from Hoboken who called themselves the Three Flashes and who already had an entrée to Bowes; Dolly Sinatra may have helped persuade the Three Flashes to expand to a foursome. The four won the audition with their innocently vaudevillian close-harmony sing-

31

ing—it was Bowes who named them the Hoboken Four—and toured the country for several months, getting all the way to the West Coast. But they were never close to start with, musically or personally, and Sinatra finally decided that he preferred the anonymity of New Jersey to the loneliness and artificiality of a Bowes tour.

The New Jersey club scene of the mid-Thirties was curiously similar to that faced by Bruce Springsteen in the Sixties and Jersey rock bar bands to this day: fairly active, but rarely leading anywhere beyond itself—the distance across the Hudson sometimes seemed infinite. The structure of the music business was rather different from what it is today, however. Popular music was dominated by the bands of the rapidly emerging swing era, by attendant singers and by "songpluggers," whom publishers hired to peddle sheet music to leading performers. The songs were cranked out by sometimes famous, more often faceless craftsmen who labored for Manhattan publishing companies, most of them working on or near Twenty-eighth Street—nicknamed Tin Pan Alley, after the cacophony of hundreds of competing upright pianos—and later in the Brill Building on Broadway. Then as now, corruption, or payola, was endemic, with the songpluggers functioning in the same way as today's independent promotion men, struggling to get their recordings played any way they can.

Sinatra's most sustained engagement came at a club called the Rustic Cabin on Route 9W in Alpine, New Jersey, where he spent eighteen months in the late Thirties singing, emceeing and, now and then, waiting on tables, all for $15 per week (later boosted to $25). But a club spot, however secure, was only a means to an end. During the swing era, every young singer's goal was to attract the attention of a bandleader and become a featured vocalist. For an unknown like Sinatra, the key was exposure on the radio, which in a few short years had challenged live performance as the primary means for publicizing popular songs, just as recordings were quickly overtaking sheet music as the preferred mode of commercial distribution. In 1920, there were two radio stations in the United States, in Pittsburgh and Detroit. Two years later there were five hundred, with nationwide networks formed by NBC in 1927 and CBS in 1928. To achieve the instantaneous exposure this new medium could bring, Sinatra was eager to donate his services—or to give up club dates if the owner proved unwilling to install a "wire," meaning a telephone line through which radio stations could pick up remote concerts for broadcast. One of the advantages of the Rustic Cabin was that it had just such a wire, and through persistence and charm, Sinatra eventually convinced the stations to let him broadcast daily, throughout the New York area, from their own studios. For this he was paid nothing at all by WNEW; at another station, in Newark, at least carfare was part of the deal.

"He was a pusher but polite," recalled Jimmy Rich, who served as station accompanist for WNEW in those days. A similar attestation to Sinatra's unique blend of aggression and grace came from the first bandleader to hire the young singer, in 1939: "His name is Sinatra, and he considers himself the greatest vocalist in the business," said Harry James. "Get that! No one's ever heard of him! He's never had a hit record. He looks like a wet rag. But he says he's the greatest!"

Sinatra's persistence in obtaining radio outlets paid off when he signed on with James at $75 per week. His first concert appearance came in June 1939; his first review, by George T. Simon in *Metronome*, followed the next month (". . . the very pleasing vocals of Frank Sinatra, whose easy phrasing is especially commendable . . ."), and his first (uncredited) recording was also made in July.

"Crooner Meets Swooner": In September 1943, Sinatra met Bing Crosby, the idol of his youth, for the first time.

**Left: With Gene Kelly in M-G-M's
1945 musical *Anchors Aweigh*,
the story of two sailors on shore
leave who help a girl extra win
screen stardom. Kelly rehearsed
Sinatra in their dance routines
for two weeks before the
cameras rolled, and the singer
later acknowledged the debt: "He
taught me everything I know."
Right: Sinatra joined Red Skelton,
Eleanor Powell, Tommy Dorsey,
Virginia O'Brien and Bert Lahr in
the 1942 feature *Ship Ahoy*.**

Above: Breaking into a spontaneous dance routine during a recording session in the early 1940s. By late 1943, Sinatra was the lead singer on the Lucky Strike Hit Parade and held the top two slots on the *Billboard* charts. At right, center, is one of his earliest sponsors, Major Bowes.

Above: Sinatra with a young
admirer. His fame placed him on
the cover of many music and
movie magazines. Right:
The face of "The Voice": "I love
you so bad it hurts," wrote one
plaintive fan on stationery
smeared with lipstick. "Do you
think I should see a doctor?"

That same year, Sinatra married his longtime sweetheart, Nancy Barbato, who eventually bore him three children and with whom, after their divorce in 1950, he has remained on warm terms. The wedding took place at Our Lady of Sorrows Church in Jersey City. "I don't want anyone dragging on my neck," Sinatra is said to have warned her, graciously. "I won't get in your way, Frank," she replied. Years later, explaining why she had never sought a new husband, she answered: "When you've been married to Frank Sinatra . . ."

James had been a star trumpeter for Benny Goodman, but in 1939 he was still a fledging bandleader struggling to find a place for himself on the teeming swing-band scene. Sinatra had the talent and ambition to go further fast, and while his records didn't sell much, his reputation spread quickly in musical circles. In six months, James released Sinatra from his contract so he could join one of the most popular bandleaders of the day, Tommy Dorsey. Sinatra sang with Dorsey from January 1940 until September 1942. It was during that period that he became a star, recording frequently and appearing in his first films with the band. He attracted so much attention, in fact, that with his emergence as a solo act in 1942, his triumph was almost a foregone conclusion. But just how triumphant, with the hysteria and artistic mastery yet to come, no one could imagine—not even the cocky young singer himself.

BY THE EARLY FORTIES, then, the first phase of Sinatra's musical apprenticeship had been completed. Except for the lush, symphonic Axel Stordahl ballad arrangements that were to become the principal backdrop of his solo period with Columbia Records after 1942, his voice and singing technique were basically established during his years as a band singer. The Fifties were to bring a refinement of that style, a sharpening of focus, and such arrangers as Nelson Riddle and Billy May were to reemphasize the swing-era jazz feeling of Sinatra's instrumental backing and phrasing. But the basis was laid with James and Dorsey. However, to understand the nature of his technique and style—what he sounded like and why—Sinatra must be placed in time, within the process of singing style as it had evolved by the early Forties.

For many years, American popular music from the nineteenth into the twentieth century was seen as a progression by which indigenous, and especially black, elements gradually supplanted European forms. This influence could be observed, many felt, in the spirituals of Stephen Foster and more generally in minstrel shows, ragtime and Dixieland jazz. But a better perspective on our past suggests that Foster and the minstrel shows evinced no more Negro influence than the idlest kind of exotic flavoring. The basic models came from Europe, either from Scottish-Irish folk song or from opera and, later on, operetta. While ragtime and Dixieland jazz drew more directly from black music, the European domination of American mainstream popular music was quickly reestablished by Tin Pan Alley. That ascendancy can be explained in musical, ethnic and economic terms.

New York was not always so central to the business of American popular music as it became early in this century; other cities had shared in the publishing of popular sheet music before then. The publishers began concentrating in New York in the late 1800s, simultaneously with the influx of Jewish immigrants fleeing pogroms in Eastern Europe. In the 1880s there were eighty thousand Jews in New York; by 1910 there were over a million. Jews came to dominate not just publishing but radio broadcasting and its West Coast entertainment extension,

As a young singer, Sinatra had consciously perfected his technique with the microphone, developing a conversational ease that helped revolutionize the popular singing of his day. He once spoke of using the mike "like a Geisha girl uses her fan."

Hollywood films. And they towered over everyone else in songwriting as well, especially for Broadway and Hollywood—a kind of songwriting that could be seen as a clear prolongation of the operetta tradition.

This tradition, with its emphasis on escapist entertainment and romantic love, was epitomized by Irving Berlin, Jerome Kern and George Gershwin. Although early on most such songs were constructed on fairly simple strophic patterns—outgrowths of the vaudeville and ragtime styles popular early in the century—they had by the mid-Twenties taken on a new sophistication of formal structure, melody and rhythm. More crucially, they had a clear dramatic shape, mirroring the narration of the lyrics by rising to a musical climax through harmonic tension and repeated melodic figurations. Except for Gershwin, who made a real effort to adapt Negro influences into his music, this sophistication remained primarily European, echoing in popular music the vocabulary of classical music of the late nineteenth century.

So, while the songs were American in their insouciant lyrics and their musical verve, along with some fashionable Negro touches, down deep they represented a reductive variant of the classical tradition, reflecting the Euro-centered tastes of their creators, performers, distributors and audiences. It was these songs, composed and published by men based in New York and appealing primarily to a white, urban, middle-class audience, that provided the raw material for the arrangements and improvisations of both white and black jazz bands between the world wars and that formed the core of Sinatra's repertory from the mid-Thirties to the mid-Eighties.

Hence, although Sinatra is a popular singer, his idiom and vocal technique are classical in origin. His "classical" style is a product of Tin Pan Alley and its own classical derivation, and of the electronically modified, jazz-inflected vocalism that emerged in American music with radio and the electrical recording process in the mid-Twenties.

Sinatra was a singer with swing bands, which are considered part of the history of jazz. But in fact they inhabited a curious netherworld between jazz as we use the term today, as an essentially improvisatory style, and unashamed pop—which, in turn, was shaped by a residual influence from classical music. The swing era, which lasted roughly from Benny Goodman's first real success in 1935 until the end of World War II, was a time of jumping brass ensembles; *Down Beat* magazine listed seven hundred of them in the late Thirties. Swing bands had evolved from stylistically similar black bands in the Twenties and early Thirties and, further back, from the Sousa-style marching bands and New Orleans brass bands of earlier decades. Such bands filled the need for large, rhythmically vivacious ensembles loud enough for dancing in noisy halls and clubs. They played mostly instrumental dance music with vocal refrains and coexisted with "sweet" bands, which featured softer music and more extended vocal solos and group harmonizing. The reason Sinatra much preferred joining Dorsey in 1940 instead of his principal competitor, Glenn Miller, was that Dorsey had a reputation for providing a more generous, deferential showcase for his singers.

The volume of such bands didn't just fill an immediate practical need; it responded to a deep-seated human desire for loud, brilliant music, both vocal and instrumental. Communal African drum sessions and clattering Chinese percussion ensembles were also responses to this desire, as was the growth of the Western symphony orchestra from the mid-eighteenth to the late nineteenth century—an expansion only partially explained by the ever-larger halls required

By 1946, Sinatra's records were selling at the rate of ten million a year. For a time, Columbia was issuing one new Sinatra record each month.

Above: A group of Sinatra fans
listening to the object of their
affections on a record player.
When Sinatra was hospitalized
for a few days with a sore throat,
some mourners wore black
bobby socks until the crisis
passed. Right: A 1940s portrait
of "The Voice That Is Thrilling
Millions": The Lean Lark, the
Croon Prince of Swing, the Bony
Baritone, Swoonlight Sinatra,
Prince Charming of the Juke
Boxes, Shoulders, the Sultan
of Swoon, Sinatra dominated
American popular music during
the war years.

Policemen with bow ties protect
Sinatra from his fans as he leaves
a train in Pasadena, California.
His wide-shouldered suits
became an important influence
on men's fashions, and by the
mid-1940s, sales of his trademark
neckwear increased 400 percent.

Left: Autograph seekers mob
Sinatra as he emerges from a
session of the Hit Parade.
Right: New York's Paramount
Theater, stormed by thirty
thousand fans during a Sinatra
engagement there, in the now-
legendary Columbus Day
riot of 1944.

by a newly affluent bourgeoisie. Similarly, the steadily rising pitch from the seventeenth century to today—a semitone higher for the standard A— reflected the public's instinctive need for brilliance and excitement.

This development toward grandiosity can also be seen in the evolution of operatic singing, which had a direct bearing on popular singing well into Sinatra's heyday—in 1945 Sinatra was replaced on the Hit Parade radio show by the Metropolitan Opera baritone Lawrence Tibbett. The most fascinating theorist of the evolution of popular singing style—if maddening for lovers of today's operatic voices—is Henry Pleasants, in his book *The Great American Popular Singers*. To simplify his thinking brutally, Pleasants argues that the development of operatic style from the seventeenth century until our time put a premium on volume and brilliance at the expense of subtlety and expressivity. The microphone enabled singers to revert to the pure principles of Italian bel canto; and hence Frank Sinatra is a "better" singer than, say, Enrico Caruso—or Tibbett.

Opera was invented in the late sixteenth century by Florentine aristocrats bent upon re-creating Greek tragedy as it was actually performed in classical times—that is, sung, although the music has been long since lost. Their ideal, which they called *bel canto*, was a flexible flow of musical declamation, with the melodic line subtly and sinuously supporting the poetic text. This purity was soon eroded by the demand for vocal brilliance and grander instrumental forces. Still, as recently as Mozart's and Rossini's time, opera singers sang far more delicately than they do today.

It was only by the mid-nineteenth century, for instance, that tenors began taking their high Cs routinely "from the chest"—in other words, booming them in a full-throated bellow—instead of floating them out with a mixture of falsetto and attenuated "head tone." By the beginning of this century, with the triumph of the blustering, impassioned verismo style of Italian opera, the quintessential operatic star was a thrilling belter like Caruso—who, it should be remembered, demonstrated the commercial viability of vocalists on the then-new phonograph records, singing both operatic arias and popular songs.

This belting style was paralleled in the operetta-influenced music that predominated in vaudeville and popular song into the 1920s, Al Jolson being its prime exponent. But by the Twenties, something revolutionary had happened to popular singing, and that was the advent of the microphone—first for radio, then for recordings, with the electrical recording process in 1925. For their live dates, singers needed amplification to compete with the more aggressive bands that were accompanying them. Rudy Vallee, one of the first pop-music idols in the modern sense, used a megaphone before turning in 1930 to a primitive kind of concert amplification—attaching an NBC carbon microphone to an amplifier and several radios set onstage, thereby duplicating in concert the parity between voice and accompaniment that could be achieved in the broadcast studio.

Amplification didn't just let singers be heard over loud accompaniments. It made possible a whole new singing style that was subtler and more intimate than quasi-operatic pop belting—and hence, Pleasants holds, constituted a welcome reversion to the original bel canto ideal. This new singing style was called crooning. It was epitomized by Bing Crosby, who had become a star with the founding of nationwide radio networks. Crooners didn't have to belt out their voices in order to reach the rafters; a microphone allowed them to float the sound easily on the breath, articulating consonants clearly and naturally.

Sinatra was fully aware of the importance of amplification. As a young singer, he consciously perfected his handling of the microphone. "Many singers never

With the Andrews Sisters, perhaps the best known of the harmony groups that flourished during the war years.

learned to use one," he wrote later. "They never understood, and still don't, that a microphone is their instrument." A microphone must be deployed sparingly, he said, with the singer moving it in and out of range of the mouth and suppressing excessive sibilants and noisy intakes of air. But Sinatra's understanding of the microphone went deeper than this merely mechanical level. He knew better than almost anyone else just what Pleasants has maintained: that the microphone changes the very way that modern singers sing. It was his mastery of this instrument, the way he let its existence help shape his vocal production and singing style, that did much to make Sinatra the preeminent popular singer of our time.

He has often talked of his concern for lyrics. In part, this means that the mood of his singing, and of the arrangements he countenances, is based on his poetic interpretation of a song's lyrics, not just on his feeling for the music. When he began to work more closely with jazz musicians in the Sixties, he encouraged them, too, to consider the lyrics before launching into improvisatory flights on the tune. Sinatra put words first in another, more basic way, however. His very manner of phrasing, how he shades the pitches of certain notes, bending and teasing the rhythm, was conditioned not just by his dramatic feeling for the words but by the way the microphone facilitated a conversational ease in his actual manner of vocal production.

Sinatra was listed as lead tenor with the Hoboken Four in 1935, but even then he was a light baritone. Over the years his voice has deepened—a process he says he welcomes, since it lends his singing a manly gravity. His mature voice is a classic baritone, the category closest in weight and timbre to a normal male speaking voice. The range is roughly two octaves, comparable to that of an operatic baritone, from the G above middle C to two octaves below that, with the whole voice slipping down a step or two as he aged (these parameters do not include his upper falsetto extension, which he would occasionally deploy in his early period for eerie final high notes).

What gives Sinatra his distinctive quality, and what makes it easier for him to declaim conversationally, is his vocal "edge"—the focused sharpness of attack that defines every note. Unlike many singers', classical or pop, his voice rarely slips back into his throat, becoming more artificially rounded in tone—some opera singers, like Joan Sutherland, swallow everything into a mush of vowels— or more gravelly and vibrato-ridden. Sinatra hardly ever lapses into the frayed hoarseness of so many rock and rhythm & blues singers, which lends them a much-prized soulfulness but sometimes also signals career-threatening nodes on their vocal cords.

Sinatra's singing is also defined by the accent he uses in conversation, a blending of his Hoboken–New York roots with broad aristocratic A's. The nasality of his singing is not just upper-class affectation, however; it is a product of the forwardness of his vocal production, the way he lets the tone resonate in his nasal cavities instead of becoming constricted in his throat and chest. In so doing, he is conforming to the finest classical operatic principles. Singing like Sinatra sings is living on interest; he hardly ever has to dip into capital.

He also subjected himself to the same sort of conditioning that opera singers put themselves through, building up his wind and his endurance with swimming and running. While he has sometimes asserted that he never had any classical training, that seems to have been a populist pose. In 1941, as a Dorsey band-member, he published a short pamphlet ostensibly coauthored by himself and his voice teacher, so identified on the cover, called "Tips on Popular Singing."

Reading the *Hollywood Reporter* Sinatra kept in touch with his second career. His films of the Forties capitalized on his All-American innocence. *Look* magazine later dedicated four pages to his first screen kiss, with Gloria de Haven, in *Step Lively.*

On the front steps of his home in
Hasbrouck Heights, New Jersey,
after a late-night club date,
and painting a chair while his
daughter Nancy plays nearby.
His well-publicized brawls and
his rumored mob connections
were deliberately countered by
such posed scenes of domestic
tranquillity.

Left: Packing a suitcase with his wife, Nancy. Extensive press coverage of Sinatra's marriage did little to discourage the romantic enthusiasm of his fans. Right: Sinatra in his dressing room at the Paramount, where he played for eight weeks in 1943; it was the longest run for any solo performer there since Rudy Vallee's in 1929.

Left: Studying sheet music in the
theater. For his more hectic radio
shows, he sometimes had to learn
songs ten minutes before air time.
He once told an interviewer,
"I wouldn't want to give anyone
the idea that I haven't worked
at this racket." Right: At the
Stork Club in 1944, with the
two Nancys in his life: his wife
and his four-year-old daughter.
According to one story, Sinatra
first became interested in Nancy
Barbato because she was the only
girl unimpressed by his ukulele
playing; they married in 1939.

Although it was probably written largely or entirely by the teacher, John Quinlan, a former opera singer from Australia, it attests clearly, in its emphasis on traditional operatic vocal production combined with a new stress on naturalness of phrasing, to Sinatra's ideas and to his direct links with classical training. The booklet is full of admonitions to avoid strain and to articulate the words naturally, along with the usual dogmatic complement of singing-manual gobbledygook ("At all times, the mouth should function with an upward and downward motion. In other words, when opening the mouth, let the jaw drop. This method produces what are known as 'dark' tones . . .").

"If it hadn't been for [Quinlan's] coaching when my voice was about gone, I'd have had no career," Sinatra later said to Earl Wilson. Sinatra also worked at times with the opera soprano Dorothy Kirsten's voice teacher, and when he encountered vocal difficulties in the mid-Seventies, after his return from a brief "retirement," he solicited the advice of the baritone Robert Merrill. To this day he follows a fixed routine of vocal exercises before each concert or recording date.

Pleasants feels that a distinguishing mark of Sinatra's vocalism is his refusal to mask the transition between the middle and upper registers, in the area of C sharp to E flat above middle C. Opera singers strive for an unbroken-sounding flow up the scale, which accounts in part for the rounded, "covered" sound they make. Remaining true to his more conversational, even folkish manner of vocal production, Sinatra sometimes reveals signs of strain in that key transitional area. But he compensates by exploiting that "weakness" for expressive purposes—a process he used to ever more telling effect as his voice aged in the Fifties, nowhere so movingly as on his album *No One Cares* from 1959.

For the purist Pleasants, it sometimes seems, the microphone should preclude any further need to sing loud or high. But this denies the human craving for the experience of effort and the thrill of physical achievement, amplified or not. Sinatra himself, by birthright, technique and preference, was never a real belter. "He is not an impressive singer when he lets out—that's a cinch," complained an early *Metronome* reviewer. As a young man, with his lighter, more tenorial voice, he could reach high notes when he had to—or even when he didn't have to: One of his first hits, "All or Nothing at All," recorded with the James band in 1939, is a sensuous ballad that he pitches comfortably in the middle of his range but with an incongruous high F tacked on the very end.

For most of his career, however, Sinatra avoided top-note display and sounded uncomfortable when a song demanded it. Even his "anthem," "My Way" (when he got understandably bored with "My Way," he began to refer to "New York, New York" as his anthem, but that was just evasive labeling), works better in the brooding introspective passages than in the surging climaxes. Sinatra's loud top notes were never secure in the operatic, proclamatory sense. Even late in his career, with audiences cheering coarsely at the climaxes, he holds something in reserve; he's almost always guardedly in control.

And yet he could achieve an anthemic effect through the sheer beauty of his legato. A 1945 recording of the Rodgers and Hammerstein "You'll Never Walk Alone" from the Broadway show *Carousel* must combat a treacly arrangement by Axel Stordahl. But the purling beauty of Sinatra's phrasing, the way he bends from note to note with the subtlest application of portamento (the Italian word for sliding gently between the pitches), builds the song to two thrilling climaxes. The beauty of that baritone, its ease and purity of texture, could never be recaptured in later years.

Not everyone felt the same way about his approach to this song. Some

61

observers assume an inherent technical inferiority of the modern microphone singer to his more stentorian predecessors and competitors. When Sinatra first visited London in 1950, the *Times* was properly appreciative of his adulatory reception by the audience and of his singing itself, except for one caveat: "When he tries his hand at songs we associate with very different singers, pieces such as 'Old Man River' and the hero's rather shaming soliloquy in *Carousel* on learning he is about to be a father, it is fair to remember that Mr. Sinatra's accomplished performance is given before a microphone. It must be easier far to 'interpret' when there is no doubt that one's voice will carry."

True, but the key word is *interpret,* not *carry,* and here we come to the style that Sinatra evolved, as distinct from physical matters of vocal production. Bing Crosby was not just Sinatra's boyhood idol and adult friend; he was a rival from whom Sinatra, as a budding solo singer, felt he had to differentiate himself. Half deliberately, half instinctively, Sinatra developed a hybrid style that represented a modification of the crooner's intimacy in the direction of a more forthright, innately Italian lyricism—a folkish tunefulness that antedated even bel canto theory in the evolution of that country's musical tradition.

In a fascinating article for *Life* magazine in 1965, Sinatra recalled his attempt to fix upon a style that would separate himself from Crosby: "I decided to experiment a little and come up with something different," he wrote. "What I finally hit on was more the bel canto Italian school of singing, without making a point of it. That meant I had to stay in better shape because I had to *sing* more."

Bel canto turns out to be a term with multiple meanings, confusingly enough. Pleasants uses it in one historically correct form, to describe the theories that brought about the birth of opera four hundred years ago. In operatic parlance today, however, the term refers to the music of Bellini, Donizetti and other Italian operatic lyricists of the early to mid-nineteenth century. Sinatra is certainly no bel canto singer in this sense. As he uses the term in his *Life* article, it means the entire Italian penchant for the heartfelt melodiousness and a vocal style suited to melodic singing. Thus, his "hitting on" bel canto was not just a clever choice; it was an instinctive response to the cultural heritage he had absorbed from his family and his ancestors—as well as an unconscious reflection of early-seventeenth-century bel canto principles.

If Jewish Americans dominated pop-music composition and publishing in the heyday of Tin Pan Alley, Italian Americans had a disproportionate impact on popular singing well into the rock era, whether their names were overtly Italian (Sinatra, Perry Como, Al Martino, Vic Damone, Mario Lanza, Julius La Rosa, Frankie Valli, Dion DiMucci, Fabian Forte, Felix Cavaliere) or not (Tony Bennett, Frankie Laine, Dean Martin, Connie Francis, Frankie Avalon, Bobby Darin, Bobby Rydell, Mitch Ryder, most of the white doo-wop groups, even the Irish-Italian Bruce Springsteen). Sinatra's own family was musical, especially his maternal grandfather, Domenico Garavanti. "Frank just grew up with lots of music around him, good music, real music," recalled his uncle, Dom Garavanti, who bought Sinatra a ukulele when the aspiring singer was fifteen years old.

The early influence Sinatra himself has most frequently cited is Tommy Dorsey's trombone playing, for its smoothness. He also mentions Ziggy Elman, who played trumpet in the Dorsey band, for his expressive application of vibrato, or the more or less rapid pulsing over a microtonal spread just around a note; and the violin playing of Jascha Heifetz, whose technically impeccable, seamlessly songful style the composer and critic Virgil Thomson once called "silk-underwear music." Dorsey was a jazz musician, and Sinatra had debts to other jazz artists,

A charity golf match arranged by Bob Hope, center, pitted Sinatra against his singing rival Bing Crosby. Sinatra carried his own golf bag, wire services reported, "giving the lie to rumors that a good gust of wind will blow him away."

Sinatra in a recording session
with the Charioteers, a gospel
group. Even at his first flush
of success, Sinatra was eager
to experiment with new musical
directions.

Although he seemed frail—he
weighed only 138 pounds—
Sinatra was a fine athlete who
often ran on the track at Stevens
Institute in Hoboken to develop
his wind and breath control.
Despite such athleticism, he
never became a vocal "belter."
His basketball technique was
limited by his height—five
feet, ten-and-a-half inches.

Left: Shortly after moving to
Hollywood, near the close of the
war, Sinatra organized his own
baseball team, the Swooners,
largely made up of his business
associates. He played second
base. Right: He was a devoted fan
of the Brooklyn Dodgers, and in
1944 sang at Ebbets Field with
manager Charlie Dressen to raise
money for the Red Cross.

too; he once said, "Mabel Mercer taught me everything I know." Above all, however, there was Billie Holiday. "With few exceptions," he wrote in *Ebony* magazine in 1958, "every major pop singer in the U.S. during her generation has been touched in some way by her genius. It is Billie Holiday, whom I first heard in Fifty-second Street clubs in the early Thirties, who was and still remains the single greatest musical influence on me." As if to reinforce this sense of fealty, he ended his last album in 1971 before what he then thought would be his retirement, *Sinatra & Company*, with a meticulously arranged, recorded and rerecorded account of the song "Lady Day." But in this early period, the influence of singers like Holiday remained subtle. It was only later, in the Sixties, that he made a real attempt to come to terms with jazz.

What Sinatra achieved when he decided to *sing* more than Crosby, and what he learned from listening to Dorsey and Heifetz, was how to sustain a legato line (in Italian *legato* means "bound," as in musical notes bound together). That was the key to smooth, melodious singing, and that was what his breath training was all about—acquiring the strength "to sing six bars and, in some songs, eight bars without taking a visible or audible breath," he wrote in *Life*. "This gave the melody a flowing, unbroken quality, and that—if anything—was what made me sound different."

It wasn't just sheer physical endurance he developed. From Dorsey, whom he saw taking little gulps of air through a "sneak pinhole" in the corner of his mouth, next to his trombone mouthpiece, Sinatra learned to inhale shallow breaths between words with a subtlety that created the illusion of an unbroken line. E. J. Kahn, Jr., the *New Yorker* writer who turned a multi-issue profile of Sinatra in 1946 into the first real book about him, even hints that he employed the Oriental technique of "circular breathing," inhaling through the nose and exhaling through the mouth at the same time, which became fashionable more recently in avant-garde jazz and classical circles.

These, then, were the roots of Sinatra's singing and style—a creative reliance on amplification to encourage a more conversational vocal idiom, combined with a determination to invest his declamation with a flowing, melodic grace. Even in his first records with James and Dorsey, bland and mewling as they often were, the Sinatra that was to come can be clearly heard. His growing prominence in the mid-Forties may have been more a matter of celebrity excitement than strictly musical accomplishment. And then, for a while, he was cruelly discarded by a fickle public. But the foundation had been laid during this early period, a firm basis on which to build during his creative explorations of the Fifties and Sixties.

The ultimate effect of Sinatra's style, fully evident in the Forties even if it was refined, enlivened and enriched in subsequent decades, is of an utter naturalness, but a naturalness attained through the devices of art. "The absence of any impression of art was imperative to his style," Pleasants wrote. "His accomplishment in avoiding it was the most compelling evidence of his stature as an artist."

SINATRA'S FIRST HIT with Dorsey, "I'll Never Smile Again," was a bouncy, sappy harmony ballad with the band and the Pied Pipers, a mixed vocal quartet of the sort common at the time. Such dreamy harmonizing, and even string sections, played a pervasive role in the swing-band arrangements, for all their brass-based dance impetus. The Pied Pipers were led by Jo Stafford, and in "I'll Never Smile Again" Sinatra periodically emerged from the group texture with solo lines of his own. The record entered the *Billboard* magazine singles chart on July 20, 1940, rose to Number One and stayed on the chart (which only contained ten discs in those days) for nearly four months. Dorsey's name was on the label, but Sinatra was on his way.

Soon he topped the influential *Down Beat* and *Metronome* polls as favorite male singer, and through 1941 twelve more of his records made the *Billboard* chart, with his own name assuming ever greater prominence in the credits. In January 1942, he cut four sides in Los Angeles with Stordahl and without Dorsey, and after that it was only a matter of time before he broke free to become a solo artist. That step was not a casual one, however; no one except Crosby had really done it successfully, and wartime posed additional, unpredictable problems. Sinatra finally made the break that summer, cutting his final record with Dorsey in July, making his final broadcast in September and his final concert appearance in October.

The parting did not come easily. Dorsey held Sinatra to his contract, which meant that the bandleader and his manager received 43⅓ percent of Sinatra's income and had a right to that amount for the next decade. At one point *Down Beat* calculated that with additional fees and taxes, 93⅓ percent of Sinatra's earnings were owed to someone other than himself, and there were giddy rumors that the figure exceeded 100 percent. Eventually, however, Sinatra and his people—Columbia Records and his booking agency—managed to buy out Dorsey and *his* people. A rumor that the mob helped convince Dorsey to release Sinatra seems less substantial than most Sinatra–mob stories, although a scene based on that allegation managed to make its way into Francis Ford Coppola's *Godfather*.

After he went out on his own, Sinatra's recordings gradually diversified from the Dorsey arrangements. The most notable changes were, at first, a spate of a-cappella recordings, several arranged by Alec Wilder, with Sinatra crooning over a cheesy-sounding backdrop of unaccompanied choral voices. The reasons for this soupiness were practical, not esthetic, even if such vocal–ensemble arrangements were part of a tradition and did manage to disfigure Sinatra recordings, off and on, for the next two decades. The a-cappella recordings came about because of a bitter strike by the American Federation of Musicians against the recording industry, which began in August 1942. Since singers were not technically bound by the walkout, this a-cappella genre flourished for a while. But eventually the singers, too, agreed to abide by the no-recording rule, and the dispute wasn't resolved until November 1944.

This recording hiatus might have crippled Sinatra's solo career at the start, at least theoretically. But the combination of his own seemingly inevitable momentum, his concert and club appearances, his press coverage, his a-cappella recordings, his first films and his radio shows—most notably as the new lead singer of the Hit Parade starting in February 1943—kept him in the public consciousness. He even managed an instrumentally accompanied hit with the rerelease in 1943 of "All or Nothing at All," which he had recorded with the James band in 1939. That year, it sold eight thousand copies; in 1943, it went over one million and placed Number Two on the *Billboard* chart, just below his version of "In the Blue of Evening."

In fact, except for the recording blackout, Sinatra launched his solo career at a propitious time—or perhaps better put, his solo success had much to do with the demise of the swing era. Bing Crosby had sustained a solo career throughout the big-band era, foreshadowing the onset of the interpretive singer's short-lived dominance in the power hierarchy of the pop-music business. Prior to that time,

Accepting donations for Russian War Relief in May 1944. Sinatra was criticized for not doing USO work in Europe until just after V–E day.

Left: During wartime, Sinatra considered it his patriotic duty to record this tune by two departed GIs. Right: Standing beneath a bomber christened with one of his nicknames. When the crew of a PT boat named their vessel *Oh, Frankie*, he sent all of them gold St. Christopher medals.

Although Sinatra was occasionally heckled by servicemen who wrongly assumed that he had been exempted from duty to preserve the fantasies of American womanhood, he was given a hero's welcome here.

Franklin Wayne Sinatra, Jr., eight
pounds, thirteen ounces, was
born at the Margaret Hague
Maternity Center in Jersey City.
Sinatra was in Hollywood making
an RKO feature, but the press
was there.

And the cameras would capture
Sinatra as he spoke to his wife on
the phone while studying a
portrait of mother and child
transmitted to the West Coast by
the Acme Telephoto Service on
January 12, 1944.

the keys to power were in the pockets of the publishers and bandleaders. Soon thereafter, in the Fifties and Sixties, financial power would shift to record-company executives and radio programmers, and creative power to singer-songwriters. But in the Forties, the strictly interpretive singer exercised an unprecedented influence; several other prominent singers also left bands for solo careers just after Sinatra did, among them Dick Haymes, Perry Como and Jo Stafford.

The principal difference in sound from the Dorsey days was the influence of Axel Stordahl, who was Sinatra's chief arranger for a decade until, in search of a new sound on a new record label, Sinatra shifted to Nelson Riddle in 1953. Stordahl was born in Staten Island in 1913 (he died in 1963) and had been a trumpeter and arranger first for Bert Bloch and then, from 1936, for Tommy Dorsey, whom he left in 1943 to work regularly with Sinatra. Stordahl's specialty, unfettered when he left the Dorsey band and had free access to whatever configuration of studio musicians he pleased, was a wash of strings and lush, neo-Tchaikovskian arrangements to accompany Sinatra's gorgeous, lyrical, intimate, introspective ballad singing. That is hardly to say, however, that novelty choral ditties and dance-oriented big-band charts disappeared altogether—far from it.

Even in the Forties Sinatra was defining what Arnold Shaw later called the "swinging ballad" and which Shaw considered a phenomenon of the Fifties, when Sinatra was collaborating with Riddle. Yet for all of Stordahl's and Riddle's importance, it was clearly Sinatra himself who shaped his sessions, and Sinatra for whom an animated lyricism represented a fulfillment of his musical instincts. "Saturday Night," recorded in November 1944, during the first Columbia instrumental session after the label finally settled with the musicians, is but one example of a big-band setting from the solo period; "Five Minutes More," from 1946, is an uptempo lyrical song. Both were Stordahl arrangements.

Sinatra has controlled his record making from the first years of his solo career. And the key to that control has been what might be called his re-creative creativity—the way he invests the apparently re-creative act of interpretation with a force of personality and musicianship that amounts to cocreation with the lyricist and composer. In an extraordinary number of cases, Sinatra's interpretations have defined the standards against which any other singer who attempted those songs had to measure himself: Sid Vicious notwithstanding, who wants to hear "My Way" from anyone except Sinatra? This kind of identification of singer and material is more common today, with the singer-songwriter. But hit songs in Sinatra's early years were commonly recorded by several singers. A popular program such as the Hit Parade was predicated on the notion that the public wanted to hear a hit *song*, not a particular singer's version of that song (indeed, in 1943–44, the singer they heard was often Sinatra, whether the song was "his" or not).

Sinatra didn't just cast a shadow over subsequent performances. He also reshaped the song in listeners' minds compared to the composer's original. It is common in jazz-inflected pop, of course, for the performer to play freely with the printed musical line. Sinatra was not the only singer to stamp his personality so completely on a song that the composer's notated version is almost forgotten. But he did it so often, so routinely, that one forgets how remarkable an accomplishment it is. The composers were not always happy with this state of affairs: Cole Porter, for one, is said to have complained about Sinatra's variations. But Alec Wilder thought that the specific melodic alterations Sinatra made in his 1947 recording of "I've Got a Crush on You" improved Gershwin's original in every case—and this despite the fact that the song probably sounds more appropriate sung by a woman.

Such a give-and-take between composer and performer was common practice in the great creative period of opera, from the seventeenth through the nineteenth centuries, when singers felt free to adapt composers' notated scores to suit their talent and their pleasure. Since Wagner, however, after the late nineteenth century, the composer has become sacrosanct, and classical music has suffered as a consequence. It can be argued that today's preeminence of the singer-songwriter constitutes an unhealthy reversion to the idolatry of the composer. While singer-songwriters have stimulated a welcome reemphasis on personal, emotional involvement in both singing and composing—a kind of expressive naturalness directly anticipated by Sinatra's own style—they have also led to a deemphasis on good singing per se. More dangerously, they have weakened the interchange that should occur between composer and performer, and encouraged compositional self-indulgence and songs circumscribed by the singer-songwriter's vocal weaknesses and idiosyncrasies.

Popular with the public and increasingly assured in his dealing with his colleagues, Sinatra was buoyed by a stylistic change in popular music between 1942 and 1947 even as he himself helped define that change. But as everyone knows, that was just part of the Sinatra phenomenon. Sinatra's fans, the bobby soxers, were so flamboyant in their affection, so boisterous in their enthusiasm, so extreme in their numbers, that they called unprecedented attention to themselves as well as to Sinatra. Other entertainers had drawn idolatrous crowds—such pop-classical "crossover" artists as Franz Liszt, Ignace Jan Paderewski, Jenny Lind and the golden-locked violinist Ole Bull. Others, most recently Rudolph Valentino, had drawn hordes of palpitating female devotees. But the pop-music idols who preceded Sinatra were either limited in their mass appeal, because electronic dissemination hadn't yet been invented, or safely sexless. Crosby appealed to an adult crowd; Frankie got the kids.

It is not entirely correct to say that those kids were *all* girls; Sinatra had his male admirers, too, and exercised a pronounced influence on male fashions of the time with his wide-shouldered jackets and big bow ties. But his fans were mostly female, and they were something. Sinatra later recalled the impact of the audience as he walked onstage at the Paramount Theater in Times Square for his first solo engagement, on December 3, 1942, as an "extra added attraction" with Benny Goodman's band. "The sound that greeted me was absolutely deafening," he said. "It was a tremendous roar . . . I was scared stiff . . . I couldn't move a muscle. Benny froze, too. He turned around, looked at the audience and asked, 'What the hell was that?' I burst out laughing and gave out with 'For Me and My Gal.' "

The initial enthusiasm soon blossomed into a national teenage love affair, which wasn't daunted in the least by the fact that Sinatra was married and, by January 1944, had a daughter, Nancy, and a son, Franklin Wayne (named for FDR, later shortened to Frank, Jr.). "The girls seem to regard Mrs. Sinatra as a cross between a godmother and an older sister," wrote E. J. Kahn, Jr. "I wish Frank were twins, one for me and one for big Nancy," said a representative fan.

The excitement, which was echoed all over the country, peaked at the bobby soxers' command center, Manhattan's Paramount Theater, in the now-legendary 1944 Columbus Day riot. The theater offered six or seven showings per day of a film, interspersed with Sinatra's appearances. There were thirty-six hundred seats, and the custom was that one could hold one's seat as long as one stayed in it.

Lighting the cigar of the world-renowned pianist, Artur Rubinstein. Sinatra downplayed his serious study of operatic *bel canto* singing, but his style captured its technique and temperament.

Left: With Moss Hart and Ethel
Merman, harmonizing in support
of FDR's fourth presidential
campaign. Presenting himself
as "a little guy from Hoboken,"
Sinatra took his political views
on the radio, as well. Right:
After his reception at the White
House on September 28, 1944,
accompanied by the legendary
New York restaurateur Toots
Shor and the film comedian Rags
Ragland. Critics of FDR publicly
asked why the president wasted
his time with a popular singer.

At work on an August 14, 1945, radio presentation with a group including Jimmy Durante, Don Lodice and Orson Welles. Jinx Falkenberg, Marilyn Maxwell, Lucille Ball and Janet Blair are seated.

Left: A song sheet from the RKO "featurette" that would win Sinatra a special Academy award. *The House I Live In* was a plea for the racial and religious tolerance he espoused during the 1940s and 1950s. Right: For all his mass appeal, Sinatra was a serious musician, who achieved an utter naturalness of style through the devices of art.

The girls would cling to their positions, chatting unconcernedly through the movie and peeing in their places rather than relinquishing their seats. "That Sinatra hits those kids right in the kidneys," an usher complained.

On October 12, at the conclusion of the first show, only two hundred fifty girls left. The trouble was, there were thirty thousand of them outside. Several bodies wide, the line extended west on Forty-third Street, north up Eighth Avenue and back east on Forty-fourth Street, clogging everything in the vicinity of Times Square. Bribing the ticket takers was one way to get into these shows, but even ticket takers couldn't accept thirty thousand bribes. Eventually, it dawned on the girls that they weren't going to get in. They vented their grief by breaking shop windows and creating an early form of Manhattan traffic gridlock. Hundreds of policemen were called in to quell the hysteria.

Pundits leapt to the attack; most of them, as they were to do again with Elvis and the Beatles ten and twenty years later, attributed precious little to Sinatra's music or his ability, through talent and originality, to thrill an audience. Instead, theories were offered ranging from his filling a void left by absent soldiers (4-F himself because of a punctured left eardrum, this was his own explanation) to mass frenzies to the primordial mothering instinct.

The most evocative recollection of what it was like to be a bobby soxer appeared in the *New York Times* in 1974, thirty years after the fact. Martha Weinman Lear lived in Boston at the time and thus gave vent to her adolescent longings at the RKO-Boston, not at the Paramount. But what she felt was shared by girls all over America: " 'Frankie!' we screamed from the balcony, because you couldn't get an orchestra seat unless you were standing on line at dawn, and how could you explain to Mom leaving for school before dawn? 'Frankie, *I love you!*' And that glorious shouldered spaghetti strand down there in the spotlight would croon on serenely, giving us a quick little flick of a smile or, as a special bonus, a sidelong tremor of the lower lip. I used to bring binoculars just to watch that lower lip. And then, the other thing: The voice had that *trick*, you know, that funny little sliding, skimming slur it would do coming off the end of a note; it drove us bonkers . . . it was an invitation to hysteria. He'd give us that little slur—'All . . . or nothing at aallll . . .'—and we'd start swooning all over the place, in the aisles, on each other's shoulders, in the arms of cops, poor bewildered men in blue. It was like pressing a button. It *was* pressing a button.

"We *loved* to swoon. Back from the RKO-Boston, we would gather behind locked bedroom doors, in rooms where rosebud wallpaper was plastered over with pictures of The Voice, to practice swooning. We would take off our saddle shoes, put on his records and stand around groaning for a while. Then the song would end and we would all fall down on the floor. We would do that for an hour or so . . .

"We were sick all right. Crazy. The sociologists were out there in force . . . What yo-yo's. Whatever he stirred beneath our barely budding breasts, it wasn't motherly. And the boys knew that and that was why none of them liked him, none except the phrasing aficionados. In school they mocked us, collapsing into each other's arms and shrieking out in falsetto: 'Oh-h-h, Frankie, I'm fainting, I'm *fainting.*' The hell with them. Croon, swoon, moon, June, Nancy with the Smiling Face, all those sweeteners notwithstanding, the thing we had going with Frankie was *sexy*. It was exciting. It was terrific."

It also couldn't last forever, and Sinatra and his press agent and de facto manager, George Evans, knew that full well. It was Evans who may or may not have hired a claque of young girls to scream on cue and trigger the rest, and who may or may not have outfitted Frankie with suits that tore apart at the slightest touch, and who may or may not have staged "chance" run-ins on the street with frenzied fans and cameramen. Any pop-music explosion occasions protests that the whole thing is a fix and a fraud; Sinatra thought just that later on about rock & roll. Whatever ingenious little games Evans was playing, he was quickly trampled by millions of fans who needed no such prompting.

Evans was also busy diversifying Sinatra's audience and media outlets. As early as March 1943, Sinatra was singing his first solo nightclub engagement, at the Riobamba in New York, which appealed to an adult crowd and which was soon followed by others around the country. He was booked with symphony orchestras: ostensibly to fundraise for them, but practically to gain adult approbation for himself. In 1943 and 1944 he was lead singer on the Hit Parade; starting in September 1945 he had his own show on CBS. And then there was his series of mostly throwaway formula Hollywood musicals for RKO and the king of the musicals heap in those days, M-G-M.

One of the first of these was *Step Lively* of 1944, in which he committed his first screen kiss, an "unprecedented bit of eroticism that," according to E. J. Kahn, Jr., "aroused so much interest that *Look*, America's Family Magazine, devoted four pages to it." The kissee was the perkily curvaceous Gloria de Haven, and at that precise moment, Sinatra reported, he realized film was "a great art medium." Also of note were *Anchors Aweigh* of 1945, the first of his three films with Gene Kelly, and *The House I Live In* of 1945, a short plea for tolerance that won Sinatra a special Academy Award.

The House I Live In was a result of his growing involvement in left-liberal causes, an involvement that seems to have been unquestionably sincere, even if it, too, was sometimes interpreted as a calculated bid for an adult audience. When Sinatra had first ventured out to Hollywood, a fresh young pop-music commodity the studios were eager to exploit, he not only had no apparent political ideas but was discouraged from the too active espousal of controversial causes. Soon, however, his social conscience was awakened, built on the base of his mother's longtime involvement in New Jersey Democratic politics. He became a firm supporter of FDR and the New Deal, visiting the White House in 1944 and actively working for Roosevelt in his fourth presidential campaign.

But by 1947, Sinatra's career had begun a five-year downhill slide that left him a seeming burnout by 1952, and his politics had something indirectly to do with that decline. An early warning sign was an engagement at the Capitol Theater in New York in November 1947. Further hoopla was anticipated, with placards reading FIRST AID STATION FOR SWOONERS, but attendance proved disappointing. The only bright spot came in retrospect. His opening act was the Will Mastin Trio, whose young star was Sammy Davis, Jr.; it was the first time Sinatra and Davis worked together professionally and, at Sinatra's insistence, the first time Davis received individual billing.

Sinatra's slippage was soon reflected in his record sales. From 1948 to 1951 he still made the *Billboard* chart, but never higher than Number Ten (in 1948 the chart had expanded to thirty songs). He declined precipitously in the annual *Down Beat* and *Metronome* polls. He lost his CBS and Mutual radio shows, and his films were poorly received, topped (or bottomed) by two turkeys of 1948, *The Miracle of the Bells*, in which he played a sanctimonious priest, and *The Kissing Bandit*, now generally regarded as his cinematic nadir.

There have been various explanations offered for this fall from public favor. Some felt there was a growing resentment against his failure to serve in the Army,

Discussing a 1946 *Metronome* all-star recording session with arranger Sy Oliver, while Johnny Hodges and Harry Carney relax between takes. Dorsey's old arranger always told Sinatra to lie back on the beat—not to push it but to let it carry him along.

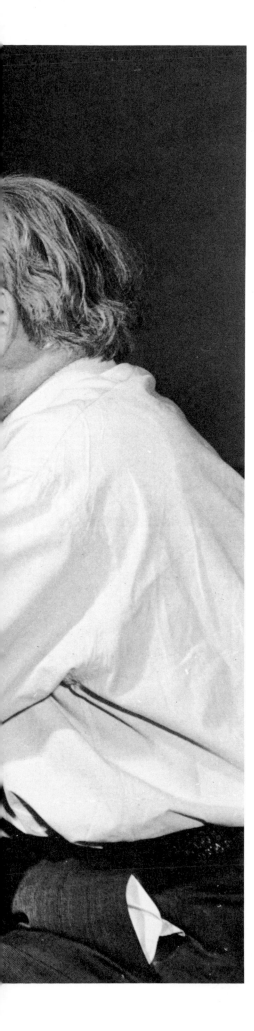

Left: The sculptor Jo Davidson
works on a bust of Sinatra that
was commissioned by *Modern
Screen* magazine in 1946. "Those
cheekbones!" Davidson cried.
"Those bulges around the cheeks!
That heavy lower lip!" Above:
The cartoonist Al Hirschfeld took
a leaner view of the singer.

Left: Waiting for the signal to begin a singing sequence in the 1946 M-G-M feature *Till the Clouds Roll By*. Sinatra's early film work was largely an attempt to capitalize on his musical fame. Right: His private life was attracting attention, as well. In the spring of 1947, he was charged with battery of a columnist, Lee Mortimer, who had allegedly called him a dago. The case was settled out of court.

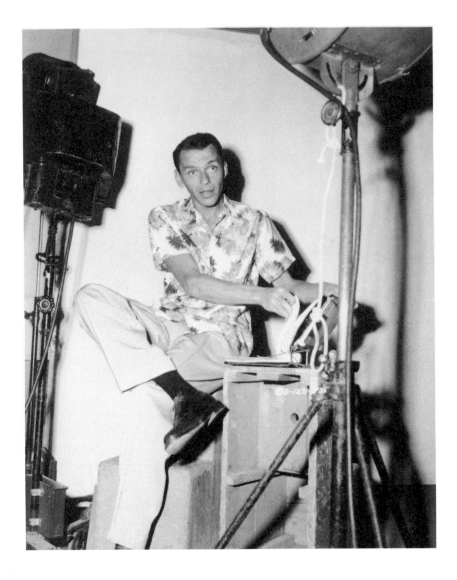

Left: From the beginning of Sinatra's film career, he was impatient with the cumbersome process of shooting a movie, convinced that he lost freshness with retakes. Right: With the former jazz pianist, now solo balladeer Nat "King" Cole, who followed Sinatra into mainstream American popular music. Sinatra turned down the song "Mona Lisa" before Cole recorded it and made it a hit.

despite his medical exemption, and of the fact that he did not undertake a USO tour until after the war was over; when he did so, he questioned the amateurishness with which the tours were organized—possibly accurate but hardly politic. "Mice make women faint, too," sniffed *Stars and Stripes*.

Another problem was his failure to capitalize on the new medium of television, on which he made his debut in 1950. Throughout the Fifties and Sixties, Sinatra had various TV series and specials, but only occasionally—as in his *Man and His Music* special of 1965—was he able to make the small screen work in his favor. Too often he allowed himself to fall victim to sloppily assembled scripts and settings, or appeared awkward and overbearing under the camera's close scrutiny.

The public seemed to be losing its taste for Sinatra the man, as well. From the first, back in the days of street scrapping in Hoboken, Sinatra had been eager to back up his opinions with his fists. Early publicity photos showed him stripped to the waist, in boxing gloves, and during the Forties he actually invested in young fighters, sometimes annoying Evans by skipping concerts in order to catch one of his charges at New York's Madison Square Garden. He had also shown a perhaps commendable willingness to defend his beliefs and his friends. Once, during a Dorsey date, he attacked a member of the audience for making anti-Semitic remarks; another time he almost got into a fight with a drunk who was throwing popcorn at Jo Stafford.

But when he became a star on his own, and especially after he began incurring enmity with the press, his barroom brawls and extramarital cavortings worked to his disadvantage. His two most publicized liaisons of the Forties were with the actresses Marilyn Maxwell and Lana Turner. But between them came a procession of dizzy blondes (and their brunette counterparts)—showgirls, hatcheck girls, minor actresses—anonymous but inimical to his fresh-faced image when splashed across the pages of the tabloids. His aura as a dutiful husband continued to fade even after the birth of a third child, Christina, in 1948.

Public disenchantment was only heightened by the first of many press reports on Sinatra's supposed socializing with Mafia kingpins. In February 1947 the columnist Robert Ruark broke the news that Sinatra had been seen drinking and gambling in Havana with the Mafia chieftain Lucky Luciano, who had called a convocation of the nation's mob leaders prior to his readmission to this country. Sinatra claimed the meetings were casual and accidental, but the damage was done.

Whether or not he was entirely straightforward in his denials, or whether he has been similarly candid in subsequent dismissals of similar charges, it is still of interest who his press enemies were, busily stoking the flames of public anger at his behavior. Many of these key opponents—Ruark, Westbrook Pegler, Lee Mortimer—came from newspapers and syndicates such as Hearst and Scripps-Howard, representing the near-rabid right and violently opposing Roosevelt, Truman, the Democrats and the New Deal. For them, Sinatra's biggest sin may well have been his outspoken support of their political enemies.

Certainly Sinatra incurred the animosity of the right. Gerald L. K. Smith, the quasi-Fascist rabble-rouser, denounced him as early as the mid-Forties. In 1949 the California State Senate Committee on Un-American Activities, a regional precursor of the McCarthy committee, named Sinatra among prominent figures who had supposedly "followed or appeased some of the Communist party line program over a long period of time."

"This statement is the product of liars, and liars to me make very un-American leaders," Sinatra replied. It subsequently emerged that Ruark's tips from Havana, and many subsequent Sinatra–Mafia stories, had been leaked to the right-wing press by Henry Anslinger, the head of the Federal Narcotics Bureau, who was convinced that Sinatra was "pink."

Politically motivated or not, the antagonism of some of the press—other foes included the columnists Hedda Hopper, Louella Parsons and Dorothy Kilgallen—was real and clearly fueled by personal animosity. The most lurid incident came in 1947, when Sinatra struck Mortimer at Ciro's in Hollywood and knocked him to the ground. Mortimer said Sinatra called him a degenerate; Sinatra said Mortimer called him a dago. Mortimer sued, and the incident was settled out of court, but not before Sinatra's name had made all the papers in an unusually unsavory manner.

In the midst of these troubles his marriage blew up in his face and the last vestiges of his image as an honorable man right along with it. Sinatra had become an almost frenzied womanizer, but in 1949 he fell in love with the woman who by all accounts was the great passion of his life, and he of hers. That woman was Ava Gardner, the green-eyed, enigmatic beauty from North Carolina who became one of Hollywood's biggest stars. They had first met in 1947, in Palm Springs, when Sinatra was dancing with Lana Turner and Gardner with Howard Hughes. The couples switched partners and, some say, Sinatra and Gardner left together.

But their real affair began two years later and, by 1950, had become so public that Nancy Sinatra was forced to file first for separation and then, after many agonizing months of indecision and legal bickering, divorce. A week after the decree was final, Sinatra and Gardner were married, on November 7, 1951, in Philadelphia. But by then the damage to Sinatra's image in those less permissive times, exacerbated by the press, seemed irreparable.

For Sinatra the musician, all these setbacks paled before one that seemed insurmountable: a sharp, multifaceted, confusing but damaging shift in the public's musical taste—and, as a direct result, the collapse of his relations with Columbia Records.

As early as the 1920s, such regionally and racially isolated forms of orally transmitted folk music as "hillbilly" and the blues had found a new form of preservation and national dissemination. Record companies—small independents or subsidiaries linked with larger companies, though still carefully segregated on separate labels—had begun to record this music. The critic Greil Marcus argues that the Orioles' "It's Too Soon to Know," played by "race" radio stations starting in August 1948, counts as the first true rock & roll record.

The late Forties was not quite the time for this music to make an overt bid for nationwide public acceptance, as Bill Haley and Elvis Presley were to accomplish just a half-decade later. Still, in this period, a slew of barely homogenized black and country records did make the mainstream charts, along with a bland form of folk music. Songs such as "Ghost Riders in the Sky" and artists such as Gene Autry, Tennessee Ernie Ford and Vaughn Monroe attested to the proto-country trend. Harry Belafonte and the Weavers sang soft but recognizable folk music.

Simultaneously, jazz was throwing off the swing era in favor of tougher, harder bebop. And in pop singing, Sinatra's smooth romanticism was being challenged by "belters" like Frankie Laine, Johnnie Ray and Eddie Fisher. They emulated black soul shouting, and along with them came such extroverted if slightly more domesticated singers as the young Tony Bennett, Rosemary Clooney, Kay Starr, Georgia Gibbs and the McGuire Sisters.

Up to a point, Sinatra found these shifting fashions stimulating. It was in the late Forties and early Fifties that he seemed most unstable in his choice of musical

Studying the music for one of his all-time favorite songs, "Laura," during a recording session in October 1947. Sinatra always made certain that the musical mood and arrangements of his songs suited his interpretation of the lyrics.

Left: For more than a decade, Sinatra collaborated with the arranger-conductor Axel Stordahl. Stordahl's specialty was a lush, neo-Tchaikovskian sound, but Sinatra ultimately shaped and controlled the results himself. Right: Relaxing with a pipe in his dressing room.

Previous page: Standing on the
Brooklyn Bridge in a scene from *It
Happened in Brooklyn* (1947);
Sinatra played a home-coming GI,
sharing the bill with Kathryn
Grayson and Jimmy Durante. Left:
Rehearsing a tune from the film
with director Richard Whorf and
composers Jule Styne, at the
piano, and Sammy Cahn, standing.
Among Sinatra's numbers was a
selection from Mozart's opera
Don Giovanni, sung in Italian. Even
these frothy musicals would make
a name for Sinatra in Hollywood.
Right: At dinner with Joan
Crawford in the late 1940s.

collaborators, restlessly shifting about in search of a style that would reflect the times and return him to the charts. But his stylistic experimentation was neither new nor a pure product of commercial desperation. As early as 1945, at the height of his first flush of success, he had cut sides with the jazz musicians Sy Oliver and Phil Moore, the Cuban bandleader Xavier Cugat and a black gospel group, the Charioteers. He had even successfully conducted an album of Alec Wilder's music in 1945—the first of several such albums, the most recent being a 1982 LP accompanying the cabaret singer Sylvia Syms. Sinatra's critically well-received conducting is all the more remarkable since he doesn't read music, or at least orchestral scores.

George T. Simon feels that some of Sinatra's best vocal work was done in 1950. Still, there were definite signs by then that taste was changing and that those changes might not work in Sinatra's favor. But he had a more immediate problem than the fickleness of the public—the autocratic policies of the man who had taken charge of his recording career.

Mitch Miller stood in the way not only of Sinatra and the integrity of his style but also of rock & roll. With all the anticipations of country, soul and folk music on the charts in the late Forties, the mass audience might have seemed ready right then for rock. Miller, who in 1950 replaced Sinatra's champion and friend Manie Sachs as Columbia's chief of recording, had helped foster the belters by signing and producing such artists as Frankie Laine. But his real predilection was for novelty numbers of a sappiness that made the Pied Pipers sound like the Sex Pistols. His taste was so silly that he seems in retrospect to have been placed on this planet for the express purpose of heralding rock's cleansing passion.

As early as 1948, George Simon reported in *Metronome* that Sinatra's "biggest gripe is the terrible trash turned out by Tin Pan Alley. 'All the popular songs of today,' he complained, 'they're so decadent, they're bloodless.' " Soon thereafter, though, Sinatra was obviously slipping and willing to cooperate with Miller, up to a point. Yet the material he was encouraged to record was of a truly dismal banality—the low point being "Mama Will Bark," a 1951 duet with Dagmar that included dog "imitations by Donald Bain." Ultimately, Sinatra came to hate Miller, and this hostility led to his leaving the label in 1952. For Sinatra, Miller became the personification of his career frustrations, the man who by foisting inferior material on him drove him off the charts.

Part of the tension between the two men derived from a struggle between entrenched and *arriviste* performing-rights organizations. ASCAP, the American Society of Composers, Authors and Publishers, had been formed in 1914 and by the late Thirties included all the best Tin Pan Alley songwriters. But a dispute with the radio networks led to the establishment, in 1940, of BMI, Broadcast Music, Incorporated. Since the best-known composers were associated with ASCAP, BMI attracted younger writers, especially those working in déclassé idioms (country, "race" and eventually rock & roll) outside the ASCAP pale.

ASCAP-oriented composers and performers such as Sinatra accused the radio networks of encouraging BMI composers in restraint of fair competition and BMI of "ruining" music. At one point, Sinatra sent a telegram to a congressional committee investigating corruption in the music business that accused Miller and Columbia of conflict of interest in favoring BMI songs. The charge seems unsubstantiated in his own case, since Sinatra continued to record a preponderance of ASCAP composers; Miller's poor taste and dictatorial tendencies were fully sufficient to explain Sinatra's difficulties with him, without invoking some darker plot. Eventually the bitterness between the two organizations abated: "My

Way" is a BMI song. But personally, Sinatra held his grudge. Years later in Las Vegas, Miller extended a hand to him in attempted reconciliation. Sinatra replied: "Fuck you, keep walking."

By the early Fifties, Sinatra had hit bottom, personally and professionally. His concerts and club dates sold miserably, with the one bright exception of a well-received London engagement in 1950. His mentor George Evans died in 1950. At a Copacabana date the same year his voice quit completely—the only time that has ever happened—and it took a period of enforced silence for it to recover. Later he joked that his penance was precisely forty days, but the memory remained seriously traumatic. Sinatra failed to register at all on the *Billboard* charts from the fall of 1951 to early 1954. One day, walking past a broadcast studio with a line of Eddie Fisher fans out front, he found himself being jeered: "Frankie, Frankie," they cried, "I'm *swooning*, I'm *swooning*." He was even reduced to groveling before his old antagonist, the press. He wrote, or had written for him, a humbler-than-thou apologia for the *American Weekly*, claiming that his temperamental outbursts had been caused by overwork and emotional strain. To the Press Photographers' Association he sent a note: "I'll always be made up and ready in case you ever want to shoot any pictures of me."

Worst of all, his marriage to Gardner had hardly calmed their tempestuous, perhaps deeply romantic but even more deeply painful relationship. They seemed unable to avoid fights; impassioned interludes only prefaced new conflicts. Sinatra was driven crazy by Gardner but couldn't live without her. "I've got problems, baby," Sinatra told Sammy Davis, Jr. "That's what happens when you get hung up on a chick." His dependence seemed to be eroding his very sense of self; in some pictures of that time, he can be seen with a weedy, sleazy little pencil mustache. He cancelled films, concerts and recording sessions (before Columbia and his booking agency dropped him altogether) in order to fly forlornly around the world to join Gardner on location—to which she had been sent, some said, as a studio plot to break up their marriage.

The best documentation of this troubled time comes, as it always does with Sinatra, on a record. On March 27, 1951, just a few weeks before he cut "Mama Will Bark," Sinatra entered a New York studio and, with Stordahl on the podium, recorded a song called "I'm a Fool to Want You." He is cocredited as the lyricist, and legend has it that he was so overwrought, he could sing only one take before rushing out into the night. Even with a sugary arrangement, this is one of the most emotionally painful, compelling pieces of singing that he, or anyone, has ever recorded.

SINATRA HAS ALWAYS BEEN A SINGER, first and foremost. But during his peak years of activity, from the early Forties into the Sixties, recordings interacted with films to fuel his fame; his success in each medium called attention to his work in the other. Nowhere is this synchronicity more evident than in the process of his extraordinary comeback in 1953.

In retrospect, one can see anticipations of his return to public favor several years before it actually happened. His 1951 film *Meet Danny Wilson* was a commercial failure, but it convinced some Hollywood insiders and, more important, Sinatra himself, that he could really act. Early in 1953, he signed with Capitol Records, a fledgling Hollywood company, although the depth of his fall can be measured by the fact that he received only a one-year contract with no advance and the stipulation that he had to pay studio costs.

Contemplating mischief with th
Singing Barber Perry Como at th
M-G-M studio barbershop in 19
Italian Americans like Sinatra
and Como had a disproportiona
impact on popular singing well
into the rock era.

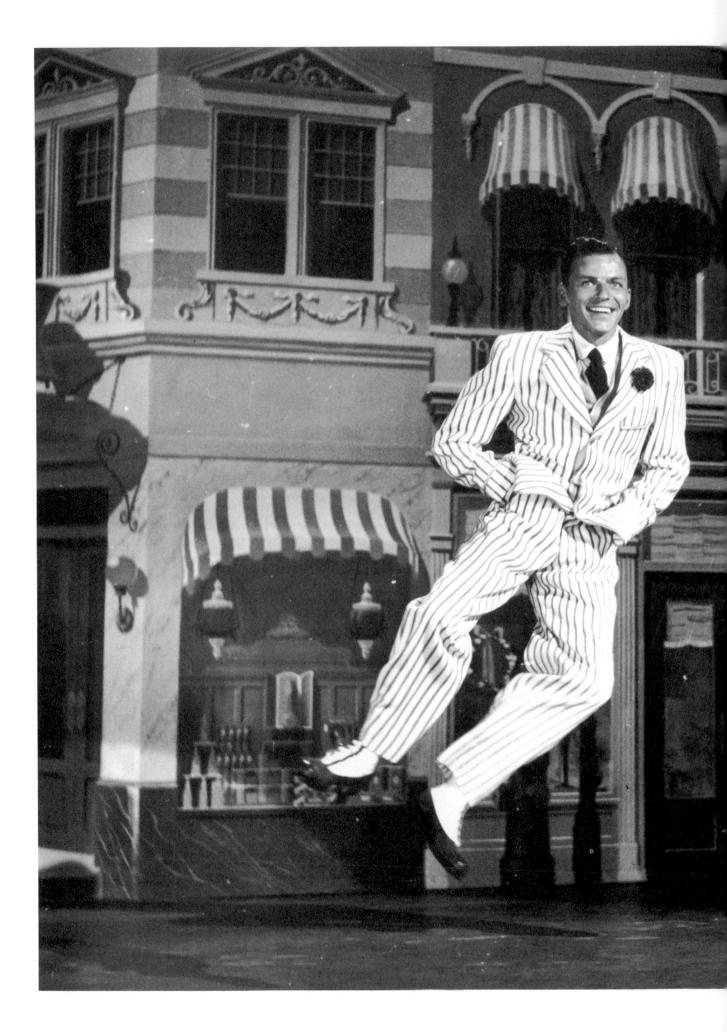

Dancing with Gene Kelly in *Take Me Out to the Ball Game*, a Busby Berkeley musical for M-G-M that also starred Esther Williams.

Left: Sinatra with his family in Hollywood in 1949: young Nancy on the swing, Frank, Jr., at right, and the baby Christina born the year before. Right: Carving the turkey at the end of the 1940s, when his time as a family man was nearing its end. Nancy would divorce him in 1951, and years later, he would remark, "She's done a magnificent job of raising the kids."

Left: On top of the Empire State Building with Betty Garrett in a scene from *On the Town*, the hit Broadway musical made into a film in 1949. Right: Waiting in an empty theater during the five-year slide that would leave Sinatra a seeming burn-out by the early 1950s. Resentment of his failure to serve during the war, disapproval of his brawls and extramarital cavortings and allegations of his underworld connections would contribute to his decline. The principal reason, however, was a shift in the public's musical taste.

But without any question, the key to his comeback was winning the part of Angelo Maggio in the film *From Here to Eternity*. Sinatra saw this feisty, ultimately heroic young soldier, with his harrowing death scene, as an ideal vehicle for a serious actor of his background. He threw himself on the mercy of Harry Cohn, the Columbia Pictures studio boss, flying back from Africa (where he had been visiting Gardner) to audition for the part, offering himself for practically nothing and waiting apprehensively until he heard the role was his. His performance, shot in March and April of 1953, won him first the excited admiration of the film community, then the plaudits of film critics and the public, and finally, as ex-post-facto certification of his new stardom, a best supporting actor Academy Award in March 1954.

By then, however, he was triumphantly back on the record charts, where he was to remain constantly throughout the rest of the decade, and almost as consistently until 1967. This new success in music was, at first, a direct result of his new celebrity as a serious film star, and of his suddenly buoyant presence in the gossip columns—no longer the compromised innocent but an adult, unashamed swinger. Sinatra's Fifties image, with his snap-brim hat, loose tie and coat thrown casually over his shoulder, became as distinctive as his other archetypal images—the wide-shouldered, floppy-pantsed, bow-tied crooner of the Forties and the gray-haired, tuxedo-clad Las Vegas elder statesman of the Seventies and Eighties.

Wherever one looked during this decade of his career, Sinatra was at work, mostly in his home base of Los Angeles but also in New York and around the world for film locations, recording sessions and concert dates. He invested a near-equal energy in his social life, with a dizzying number of casual and not-so-casual girlfriends: Among those with whom he was linked in the press were two socialites, Gloria Vanderbilt and Lady Adele Beatty, and the actresses Anita Ekberg, Marilyn Monroe and Lauren Bacall after the death of her husband and his friend, Humphrey Bogart, in 1957. Sinatra's stormy marriage to Gardner ended with a separation in 1953, although, with tentative attempts at reconciliation by Gardner (abetted by Sinatra's mother Dolly), the divorce did not take place until 1957. Sinatra remains on good terms with Gardner, as he does with his first wife.

However much his social life bolstered his public reputation, the two pillars of Sinatra's career remained films and music. After his success in *From Here to Eternity*, Sinatra felt driven to prove that his suddenly recognized acting skills were no fluke. But he was also eager and willing to cash in on his new success. Throughout the Fifties, he was incessantly active, so feverishly so that on the set of *High Society* in 1956, his and Bing Crosby's nicknames were Dexedrine and Nembutal. Five Sinatra films were released in 1955, including *The Tender Trap*, *Guys and Dolls* and *The Man with the Golden Arm*.

Seen as a whole, Sinatra's film career describes an arc up from innocently exploitive musicals of the Forties to the serious films of the Fifties and back to a harder, tougher cynicism in the Sixties. In the Forties, first with the Dorsey band and then on his own, Sinatra was thrown—he volunteered, of course—into the formula-musicals machinery of the day. This sort of musical, not much more ambitious than today's television films, represented an automatic extension of the same sensibility, and often the same people, as the Tin Pan Alley musical world of New York.

In the short run, films served as promotions for concerts, radio shows and records; they were the rock videos of their day. Films were meant to make money on their own, of course, for the studios and for Sinatra. But they were also a form of career diversification, another way of opening up the young star to an adult audience, of shoring up his success against the inevitable fading of his fad—certifications of celebrity for an adult world that never took youth music seriously. As with Elvis a decade later, Sinatra went into films because that was what a youth idol was supposed to do. Whether or not he could act was completely beside the point.

It was easier for a young singer to move into sound films than it would have been a few years before to star in silent films (where the emphasis was on emotive facial expressions) or on the legitimate stage (with its orotund acting tradition). The sound-film camera had an impact on acting similar to that of the microphone on singing. Both undercut the need for booming projection and favored a subtler, more naturalistic style. And both circumvented the requirement of a laboriously accrued, artificially inflated technique.

For Sinatra, who had always stressed the importance of lyrics in conveying the dramatic essence of a song, the transition from song to screen was more natural than the other way around. "Actors who can't sing can't switch to our side," he said at the the time of his 1954 film, *Suddenly*. "But there's no reason why a singer can't go dramatic. A singer is essentially an actor." Sinatra's comment suggests that he had a vastly higher respect for, not to say knowledge of, singing technique than acting technique.

In his early films, Sinatra seemed to rely on what might be called the unselfconscious projection of self. This technique, if it can be called that, is hardly limited to singing actors; John Wayne made himself into a legend using it. But with *Meet Danny Wilson, From Here to Eternity* and some of his subsequent films, Sinatra graduated into real acting, mastering an impressive range of characters and emotions within those characters.

His best films were in the Fifties. Before that, he was cast mostly in musicals, the liveliest of which, *Anchors Aweigh* of 1945 and *On the Town* of 1949, costarred Gene Kelly, who dominated the proceedings despite Sinatra's own onscreen charm. Kelly taught Sinatra how to dance in the course of these films. It was the most sustained period of actual nonsinging craftwork Sinatra ever indulged in, and he remembered it subsequently with enormous gratitude. His appreciation of his apprenticeship with Kelly makes one wonder what might have happened had he been similarly inspired to perfect the craft of acting.

From 1953 on, he had several meaty parts in such dramatic films as *Suddenly* (1954), *The Man with the Golden Arm* (1955) and *The Manchurian Candidate* (1962). There were also comedies—*The Tender Trap* (1955) and *A Hole in the Head* (1959)—and good, or at least starry, musicals: *Guys and Dolls* (1955), *High Society* (1956), *Pal Joey* (1957) and *Can-Can* (1960). After that, the quality declined. There were four vehicles for his gaggle of show-biz pals called the Clan: *Ocean's Eleven* (1960), *Sergeants Three* (1962), *Four for Texas* (1964) and *Robin and the Seven Hoods* (1964). They made money but were roundly panned by the critics. After 1970, the films dwindled away to nearly nothing: There was only a television movie, *Contract on Cherry Street* (1977), and *The First Deadly Sin* (1980). As of 1984, further film projects remained in the rumor stage, including the possibilities of playing a psychiatrist and, amusingly enough, Walter Winchell. But nothing seemed firm.

Sinatra's own explanation for this decline in quality and then quantity was that the scripts simply weren't there, a complaint echoed in his subsequent difficulties finding suitable new songs. But the real problem was his ongoing indifference to the very process of filmmaking—it must have been the process, because by the early Sixties he had won a large measure of control over his films, coproducing most of them and, in the case of *None But the Brave* (1965), directing as well.

With Ava Gardner, the green-eyed, enigmatic beauty who enthralled Sinatra in the early 1950s. Their relationship was passionate yet painful; Sinatra told Sammy Davis, Jr., that there was nothing worse than being hung up on a woman.

Left: Sharing the wedding cake
with Gardner after their
marriage in Philadelphia on
November 7, 1951. In those less
permissive times, Sinatra's
divorce and remarriage seriously
damaged his reputation. Right:
Sinatra and Gardner on their
honeymoon, strolling along a
beach. They would separate in
the fall of 1953 and divorce
in 1957.

With Dagmar during the May 10, 1951, recording session of "Mama Will Bark," which included dog imitations by Donald Bain—the worst of the dismal banality that Mitch Miller foisted on Sinatra at Columbia Records.

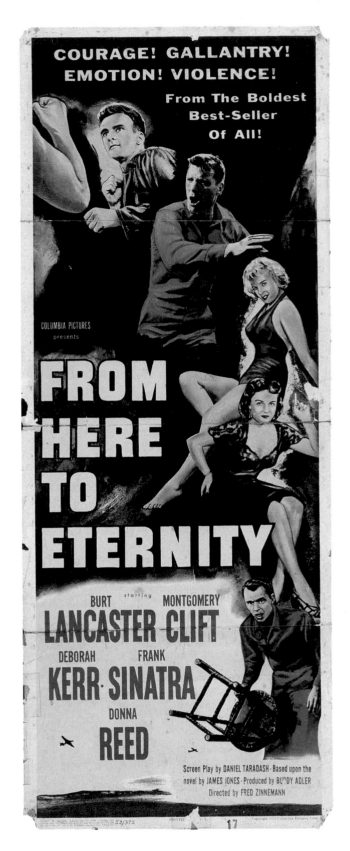

COURAGE! GALLANTRY! EMOTION! VIOLENCE!

From The Boldest Best-Seller Of All!

COLUMBIA PICTURES presents

FROM HERE TO ETERNITY

starring

BURT **LANCASTER** MONTGOMERY **CLIFT**

DEBORAH **KERR** FRANK **SINATRA**

DONNA **REED**

Screen Play by DANIEL TARADASH · Based upon the novel by JAMES JONES · Produced by BUDDY ADLER Directed by FRED ZINNEMANN

Left: In *From Here to Eternity*, Sinatra played a tough, wise-cracking, Italian-American soldier, Angelo Maggio—and proved that he could carry a powerful dramatic role. Right: The film won him an Oscar, being presented by Mercedes McCambridge, and became the key to the resurrection of his career.

One difficulty was that he seemed to typecast himself. In the Fifties, he had proven his ability, against enormous initial skepticism from the movie industry, to play a wide range of parts, from singing male ingenue to action hero to scrappy underdog to cowboy to drug addict. But since the Sixties he has tended to revert to the role of hard-bitten gangster or cop. While such parts may have reflected his boyhood fascination with gangsters and gangster films, and may have seemed relatively easy to act, they hardly encouraged a maximum effort by a star who had grown increasingly impatient with the laborious tedium of filmmaking.

From the first, the high-strung Sinatra had been impatient with the cumbersome process of shooting a film, convinced that he lost freshness with retakes and hence doing everything possible to avoid them. "I don't buy this take and retake jazz," he told Arnold Shaw. "The key to good acting on the screen is spontaneity—and that's something you lose a little with each take."

Such an attitude often put him at odds with other actors who preferred to work over their scenes repeatedly until they got them right. He was especially impatient with Method actors in general and Marlon Brando in particular. Brando was already a rival when he beat out Sinatra for the lead role in *On the Waterfront*. "Don't put me in the game," he told Joseph L. Mankiewicz, the director of *Guys and Dolls*, "until Mumbles is through rehearsing."

"Frank . . . is about as naturally talented as anybody I've ever known in my life," said Shirley MacLaine during the filming of *Can-Can*. "His potential is fantastic. The thing is, I wish he would work harder at what he's doing. I don't think when you polish something you can help improve it. He won't polish. He feels polishing might make him stagnant. He doesn't even like to rehearse. Now I don't mind that because he and I have such a rapport . . . But other actors and actresses can't always react to him that way."

Sinatra's "range and vitality as an entertainer are a phenomenon," wrote Bosley Crowther of the *New York Times* in 1967. "That's why it is so provoking— nay, disturbing and depressing beyond belief—to see this acute and awesome figure turning up time and time again in strangely tricky and trashy motion pictures." "Why has Sinatra not developed the professional pride in his movies that he takes in his recordings?" asked Pauline Kael that same year.

"Once you're on that record singing, it's you and you alone," Sinatra explained, as if in response, to the British writer Robin Douglas-Home. "If it's bad and gets criticized, it's you who's to blame—no one else. If it's good, it's also you. With a film it's never like that; there are producers and scriptwriters and hundreds of men in offices and the thing is taken right out of your hands."

The worst of his later films was probably *Dirty Dingus Magee* (1970), the movie that presaged his seven-year screen retirement. "He seems ineffably bored and totally uncommitted, as well he might be," complained Arthur Knight in the *Saturday Review*, echoing the critical consensus. "A Sinatra film never reached down into the darkness the way the songs did," wrote Pete Hamill. "He never cheated on songs."

Films were vital to Sinatra's transcendence of mere stardom into superstardom—a word debased through overuse but applicable in his case. But what certifies his importance for posterity is his singing, not his acting; his records, not his films. Music has always remained Frank Sinatra's artistic center. In his Coldwater Canyon home in Los Angeles between 1955 and 1964 there was a motto in his den adapted from Schopenhauer: MUSIC IS THE ONLY FORM OF ART THAT TOUCHES THE ABSOLUTE. Music was his psychiatrist and his priest, purging him of tensions and restoring his sense of self. "Singing was like a lightning rod,

With the heiress and actress Gloria Vanderbilt at a Broadway opening in December 1954. By the mid-1950s, Sinatra had emerged as an unabashed swinger, his name linked with a number of socialites and movie stars. Vanderbilt denied the rumors of romance, but gossip columnists noted that it was their second night together in a row.

particularly when he was in good voice," recalled Dave Cavanaugh, his Capitol producer from 1958 to 1961. "It discharged the hostile electricity."

The Fifties marked not only Sinatra's peak as a record-seller but also his finest, deepest work in the recording studio: Chart success and artistic excellence are not always synonymous in popular music, but they were here. Sinatra's first Capitol session, on April 2, 1953, was with his old arranger Axel Stordahl. But his second, on April 30, paired him with the conductor-arranger with whom he would make more great records than with any other collaborator. That was Nelson Riddle, a fellow New Jerseyite, born in 1921, a former trombonist for Tommy Dorsey. Later that year, on December 9, 1953, the two recorded a song by Johnny Richards and Carolyn Leigh called "Young at Heart"—one of the few in Sinatra's career, he later wrote, that had literally "come in over the transom." This buoyant ballad entered the *Billboard* singles chart on February 13, 1954, rose to Number Two and stayed on the chart for over five months.

But while Sinatra remained a fixture on the singles charts for several years to come, his real success coincided with, and was propelled by, a shift in the record-buying habits of the public. The LP disc—at first usually ten inches, later the now-standard twelve inches—was introduced in 1948. But it was not until the early Fifties that it began to challenge the single as the preferred medium for pop-music recordings, gradually supplanting the single in dollar volume and becoming the index by which a recording artist's success was measured.

The audience for singles has always preferred lively dance tunes and, by the late Fifties, that meant rock & roll. Singers who do their best work in ballads count on album buyers to appreciate them, and that is why the shift in emphasis from singles to albums was so important to Sinatra's career longevity. He had never been entirely comfortable within the confines of the three-minute pop song, and on an album, he could build a mood, fast or slow, and sustain it. As an interpretive singer, he himself couldn't create musically interlocking statements. But his preference for upbeat or ballad collections, usually linked by a single theme (*Come Fly with Me, Songs for Swingin' Lovers*), led the critic Stephen Holden to assert that he pioneered the "concept album."

By the mid-Fifties, the refocusing of his attention from singles to albums was complete. From 1957 until 1966 he had no Top Ten *Billboard* singles, but he did have twenty-seven Top Ten albums. His first Capitol album (ten inches), *Songs for Young Lovers*, entered the album chart two weeks after "Young at Heart" made *its Billboard* debut. The apex of his commercial ascendancy came in 1958 and 1959. In the first year, he had the top two albums of the year in *Come Fly with Me* and *Only the Lonely*; in 1959, *Only the Lonely*, which had entered the charts in September 1958 and stayed there for one hundred twenty weeks, was competing with *Come Dance with Me*, which joined it in early 1959 and remained for one hundred forty weeks.

To assert the superiority of Sinatra's Fifties recordings is not to undervalue the best albums from his years with Reprise after 1961, many of which hold up admirably on song-by-song comparisons. But the balance of youthful resources and mature experience, a set of unequaled collaborators and a period in pop-music taste most receptive to his music combined to create a magisterial body of work.

From a technical standpoint, Sinatra's voice had deepened and darkened slightly, coarsening the mellowness that had marked his recordings from the Dorsey days. At the same time, the slight insecurity in the area just above middle C became more pronounced, and Sinatra was masterful in exploiting that frailty for expressive purposes. He realized, and made his listeners realize, that his voice

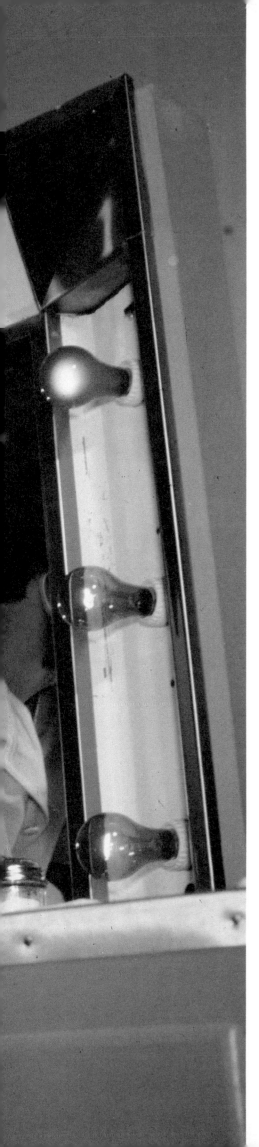

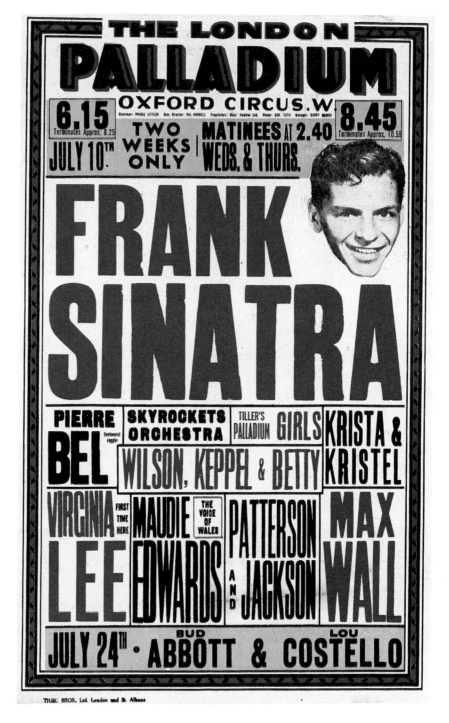

Left: On a doughnut break in his dressing room. Between 1955 and 1956, Sinatra would appear in nine films, mastering an impressive range of characters and becoming a major box-office draw. Above: By now his fame had spread worldwide; beginning in July 1950, he performed a series of concerts at the London Palladium.

During the shooting of *Guys and Dolls* in 1955. Every day on the set, Sinatra sent out for Italian food to avoid the commissary fare, then invited the actors and his collection of hangers-on.

Left: *Guys and Dolls* was the story
of a small-time hood named
Nathan Detroit who ran a crap
game for the hotshot gamblers in
town. The role was a natural for
Sinatra, whose self-image was
shaped, in part, by the gangster
films of the 1930s. Right: Sinatra
would produce the first film of
his own, *Johnny Concho*, in 1956,
modeled on the Hollywood
westerns he had long admired.

had taken on new physical attributes to compensate for the loss of youthful beauty.

But it was more the musical skill with which Sinatra deployed that voice, and the overpowering image he created—an image to which his films, his television shows, his radio broadcasts and not least his well-publicized private life all contributed—that invested his music with its last degree of dangerous allure. If the bobby soxer Sinatra had thrilled adolescent girls with his slithering portamento, his spitcurl and his boyish smile, the grown-up Sinatra gave off a more potent, mature sexual allure. He invested uptempo songs with a new punch and swagger, attaining an irresistible energy through rhythmic attack rather than belting overkill. And he was supported by a jazz feeling both subtler and more pronounced than in his Stordahl period.

His ballad singing had improved as well, on both musical and emotional terms, lending him a new vulnerability that mirrored the cocky aggression of his upbeat material. Ava Gardner may have left scars, but as happens so often with great artists, personal pain translated into artistic achievement. As proof, one need only turn to one of Sinatra's first Capitol albums, *In the Wee Small Hours*, the first side of which offers the following sequence: "In the Wee Small Hours of the Morning," "Mood Indigo," "Glad to Be Unhappy," "I Get Along Without You Very Well," "Deep in a Dream," "I See Your Face Before Me," "Can't We Be Friends" and "When Your Lover Has Gone." A public that had at first been titillated, then offended, by the Gardner–Sinatra relationship was now ready to recognize its validity once they heard it expressed as poignantly and painfully as this. At the same time, Sinatra himself seemed to have gained a new, deeper dimension by this harrowing affair.

Allied to his new emotional intensity was a more artful articulation of the naturalness that had always defined his singing style. The final vestiges of sentiment and rhetoric seemed to have been burned out of his singing, leaving only the most direct expression of emotion. This accomplishment is all the more remarkable when one considers that all around him, even in his inner circle, the Tin Pan Alley style was rapidly devolving into what we now call "middle of the road," or schlock. The truest standard of comparison is not with such panderers of latter-day middle-of-the-road bombast as Engelbert Humperdinck and Barry Manilow, but with Sinatra's peers and competitors. There were those who sang as mellowly as he (Crosby, Como), with more jazz virtuosity (Vaughan, Fitzgerald), as insouciantly (Tormé), as dramatically (Bennett). But Sinatra best combined these virtues into one sharply focused sensibility, and he nearly always managed to pare away the affectations that date other singers of his generation while retaining a natural contemporaneity. Sinatra foreshadowed the emotional veracity of the best rock without being directly akin to it. Lord knows, rock has its inflated, bathetic, overrhetorical side, too. But much of it, hard or soft, speaks within the conventions of conversational "sincerity," and Sinatra was doing that before today's crop of rockers was even born.

His albums from the Fifties reaffirm one more thing—the ability of a strictly interpretive singer to make as purely personal a statement as any singer-songwriter. Nearly all performing musicians, one-man synthesizer bands possibly excepted, must collaborate, but interpretive singers must collaborate more than most. They rely on composers for material, arrangers and instrumentalists for support, producers for recorded ambience. Yet the best of them, and Sinatra is the very best of all, project a personality that infuses their work, transforming songs by others into the most immediate of individual statements.

At the "wrap" party for *Johnny Concho*. Sinatra brought a small jazz combo onto the set and presented an individual portrait to each member of the cast. He was always known for such flamboyant generosity.

Of all a singer's collaborators, the most crucial are "his" composers, meaning those he selects and surrounds himself with, commissioning and inspiring. All his performing life, Sinatra's principal musical mission has been to preserve, protect and enliven the great Tin Pan Alley songs of the Twenties, Thirties and Forties—music by such men, each central to his repertory, as Berlin, Gershwin, Porter and Rodgers. But he has also associated himself with songwriters he hoped could prolong that idiom: Sammy Cahn, Jule Styne, Jimmy Van Heusen and Johnny Mercer are lyricists and composers who figure prominently in his repertory and in his circle of friends as well; he even shared bachelor quarters with Styne in 1954. In later years, he and his associates lost touch with contemporary idioms, a process that culminated in Gordon Jenkins's inflated "cantata" that makes up the final record of his three-disc album of 1980, *Trilogy*. But in the Fifties, the atrophy wasn't yet apparent, and Sinatra's taste in songs both old and new, his feeling for a number with a good melody, sophisticated lyrics and, above all, a meaningful narrative line, seemed well-nigh unerring.

Riddle was the key to Sinatra's Capitol sound, the model against which all his other arrangers then and since must be measured. What Riddle offered was a sure sense of the swing-jazz sound from which Sinatra had emerged, a subtly masterful command of symphonic scoring, an understated ability to capture a song's dramatic essence with instrumental touches, and beyond all that, an irreducible individuality. His "swinging" records with Sinatra offer jazzish drive without untoward brassy vulgarity. But where Riddle really comes into his own is with ballads, the lush moodiness rarely overstated or sentimentalized (as with Stordahl before him and Jenkins after him) yet all the more moving for its very sparseness. And he was able magically to blend fast and slow, underpinning a ballad with insinuating rhythmic impetus, thereby combining Sinatra's two main interpretive inclinations, sexual insouciance and emotional vulnerability.

The other principal arranger of this period was Billy May, who was more overtly jazz-oriented than Riddle. May had been a trumpeter and an arranger for Charlie Barnet and Glenn Miller, and his charts for Sinatra reflect the tougher side of swing. As a result, he appears mostly on Sinatra's swinging albums, while the third mainstay, Jenkins, was used primarily for ballad sessions.

Sinatra has always cultivated his musicians, both classically trained orchestral players and such jazz soloists as Harry "Sweets" Edison, the Count Basie trumpeter who can be heard on so many of the Fifties recordings. His pianist for twenty-five years, Bill Miller, was another key to Sinatra's consistency. And the contract musicians he used, both in New York and in Hollywood, were also the best available. In Los Angeles, regular session musicians were often Los Angeles Philharmonic members picking up additional income and equally talented or superior freelancers who had gravitated to Southern California in search of sun, studio income and the Central European immigrant community that flourished there. Among others, there is the complete Hollywood String Quartet, billed as such on Sinatra's *Close to You* album but appearing individually as part of the string complement on numerous orchestral sessions. Felix Slatkin, its first violinist, is often the concertmaster and even conducted occasionally—including six numbers on *Only the Lonely* when Riddle couldn't be there.

The last link in the collaborative chain at Capitol was the record producers. Since Sinatra relied so heavily on his conductor-arrangers, the producers, Voyle Gilmore (1953–58) and Dave Cavanaugh (1958–61), had less to do creatively than many a modern-day rock, soul or country producer, who can completely control a session, from song selection onward. But their role was more custodial

With Dinah Shore on "The Chevy Show" in 1956. During the 1950s Sinatra hosted his own television series, but his blunt, aggressive personality never adapted well to the small screen.

Left: An unbilled performance in
Meet Me in Las Vegas (1956), in
which Sinatra also appeared
pulling the handle on a slot
machine. He hit the jackpot.
Right: The same year, he played
a freewheeling bachelor in *The
Tender Trap*, with half a dozen
girls on the string. He would
finally be ensnared through the
wiles of Debbie Reynolds.

Previous page: Sinatra as Barney Sloan, the bitter misfit of *Young at Heart* (1955), in a scene that could almost be a dramatic reconstruction of his resigned ballad, "One for My Baby (And One More for the Road)." Left: By now his voice had coarsened and, to compensate, he would cultivate a new, more vulnerable, emotional intensity. Right: But he had hardly lost the verve of Tin Pan Alley and sang a number of Cole Porter numbers in *High Society*, a 1957 remake of *The Philadelphia Story* costarring Grace Kelly.

for another reason, too: Sinatra retains far greater control over his recording sessions than most musicians. As on a film set, he can be impatient in the studio. He has no use for rock's endless overdubs, preferring to record live before an audience of friends and associates. But within his own terms, he retains a single-minded dominance over his recordings that he could never achieve with his films. And he is still very much a perfectionist, insisting on new takes and new ways to interpret a song, ruthlessly rejecting recordings that everyone else admires. Thus, Gilmore and Cavanaugh were concerned primarily with organizing the logistics and establishing the mood in which creativity could occur. They clearly did their job well, since both were associated with some of the greatest Sinatra albums.

Individual tastes vary, of course, but there is a surprising consensus among Sinatra enthusiasts that the best of his albums from the Fifties, one from the uptempo side of the fence and one made up entirely of ballads, were *Songs for Swingin' Lovers* and *Only the Lonely*. Both, not uncoincidentally, were arranged by Riddle and recorded in Hollywood; the former was produced by Gilmore, the latter by Cavanaugh, his first full album for Sinatra.

Songs for Swingin' Lovers was recorded in October 1955 and January 1956. It may be a "swinging" collection, but it epitomizes Riddle's ability to soften the brassiness of such arrangements; most of the punchy brass interjections, for instance, are literally muted. Even the occasional ballad, such as "We'll Be Together Again" (a BMI song by Frankie Laine and Carl Fischer), gets a jazzish rhythmic underpinning.

Sinatra's singing on this album has a verve and conviction that make his records from the Forties sound bland. He has learned to tease and twist a vocal line without violating its integrity. By now, he knows how to kick forward a song's rhythmic impetus by the percussive articulation of key one-syllable words—the *such* at the outset of the first song, for instance, the very title of which, "You Make Me Feel So Young," suggests the association in Sinatra's mind between youthful energy and his swinging idiom. The album as a whole breathes with a delightful blend of Riddle's naughty sweetness and Sinatra's witty bravado—as in the counterbelting conclusion to the last song, Porter's "Anything Goes," where instead of reaching up for a Manilow-like top note, he plummets giddily down to a low E.

Only the Lonely, recorded in May and June 1958, is Sinatra's greatest album— the quintessential combination of deeply emotional songs, telling arrangements, youthful vocal resources and interpretive maturity. That is not just my opinion, but his: Asked at a New York party in the mid-Seventies if he had a favorite among all his recordings, he unhesitatingly chose this one. The album's excellence does not encompass its visual design, even if it did win a Grammy in 1959 for best album cover. The jacket comes adorned with a clown portrait of Sinatra's face, a maudlin touch reflecting his own predilection for clowns when he himself paints. On the back of the LP is another of Sinatra's recurrent visual motifs, a lamppost.

Sinatra's song selection on this album is nearly flawless: a sequence of brokenhearted torch songs that are never gratuitously depressing or unvariegated in their gloom. There are wonderful songs by fine songwriters, either older masters of American popular music or younger men linked directly with Sinatra's circle ("Spring Is Here" by Rodgers and Hart, the title tune by Cahn and Van Heusen, "What's New" by Bobby Haggart and Johnny Burke, "Goodbye" by Jenkins, "Blues in the Night" by Harold Arlen and Johnny Mercer, and "Guess I'll Hang My Tears Out to Dry" by Cahn and Styne). Some critics have groused

For ballad sessions, Sinatra would often call on Gordon Jenkins, who specialized in lushly romantic arrangements.

that Robert Maxwell and Carl Sigman's "Ebb Tide," with its atmospheric sentimentality, constitutes an intrusion into the otherwise consistent mood of adult resignation. But it seems appropriate enough to me.

Riddle's arrangements are the quintessence of his ballad style, applying pastel daubs of instrumental color only but always when necessary. The album is shot through with piano (Miller) and strings, but when other instruments solo, you remember them: the trombone in "What's New," the woodwinds in "Goodbye." One strong but characteristically subtle touch is a rising, then falling, contrapuntal wind line to a single phrase—"No desire, no ambition leads me"—in "Spring Is Here" (the song was deleted when the album was rereleased in stereo, along with "It's a Lonesome Old Town"). The winds intertwine with a chamber delicacy that Mahler wouldn't be ashamed of.

As ever, though, it is Sinatra's singing that makes this album great. For those interested in such details, he "covers" one high note with an operatic artificiality, an F in "Ebb Tide." But elsewhere, this is Sinatra singing at his intimate, vulnerable, conversational best, the voice suffused with an almost unbearable, tremulous fragility. If the "swinging" records symbolize youth, then these ballad collections herald the onset of age: *Songs for Swingin' Lovers* led off with "You Make Me Feel So Young"; here, in "Angel Eyes," by Matt Dennis and Earl Brent, Sinatra refers sadly to "my old heart."

"Angel Eyes" is a drinking song, and another such song, perhaps the greatest of all of Sinatra's torchy lamentations and as intense and true a performance as any he has committed to disc, ends *Only the Lonely*. The song is "One for My Baby (And One More for the Road)," composed by Mercer (lyrics) and Arlen (music) for a 1943 film, *The Sky's the Limit*, where it was sung by Fred Astaire; Ida Lupino also had a memorable version in a 1948 film, *Road House*. Sinatra recorded it three times. His first version, with Stordahl in 1947, is innocently balladic; it sounds sweet but almost astonishingly callow next to this 1958 performance. The last version, from the *Sinatra at the Sands* live album, dates from 1966; although the album is a collaboration with Count Basie and his orchestra, arranged and conducted by Quincy Jones, "One for My Baby" is done as a piano solo with Bill Miller, an honorable but coarser reworking of the version from 1958. The 1958 performance, incidentally, forms the centerpiece of Twyla Tharp's Sinatra ballets.

In the song the protagonist is addressing a bartender, Joe, who remains silent throughout, sympathetic or indifferent, in the time-honored manner of his profession—part psychiatrist, part confessor and part God. The singer has love troubles, bad ones, but he never overdramatizes himself or tries to get us to wallow with him; his reticence suggests the pent-up intensity of his passions. He never even tells just exactly what has happened; by alluding to the plot without actually revealing it, his story becomes everyone's story. The mood is forlorn and alone, yet it rises to an emotionality in the final chorus that is all the more painful for its very muted helplessness.

Structurally, "One for My Baby" is a sophisticated song. It is built in the standard AABA chorus form, meaning a section repeated, a contrasting passage (the *release* in Tin Pan Alley terminology, the *bridge* in rock) and a final return to the first section. This form is central to Western art music of the past two hundred years, most clearly in the "sonata form" that provides the organizational principle for the first movements of most symphonies. It is not simply arbitrary; the idea of statement, repetition with variation, contrast or development and recapitulation evolved naturally to reflect the basic human emotional need for variety and reaffirmation.

With Billy May, one of Sinatra's principal arrangers during the 1950s. A jazz-oriented trumpet player, May would bring a tough vivacity to the swinging albums.

Left: Sinatra sang the classic
"The Lady Is a Tramp" in *Pal
Joey* (1957), which costarred
Kim Novak and Rita Hayworth.
Right: Novak, Sinatra, Lauren
Bacall, Humphrey Bogart and Mrs.
Gary Cooper. Sinatra's close-
knit entourage, the Clan, grew
out of Bogart's Rat Pack
in the mid-1950s.

A recording session attended by
Lauren Bacall and Sophia Loren.
Sinatra preferred to record live
before an audience of friends and
associates.

Left: Greeting Nikita Khrushchev
on the set of *Can-Can* during the
Soviet premier's visit to the
United States in 1959. With
Sinatra are the film's other stars,
Louis Jourdan, at left, and Shirley
MacLaine. Right: At Puccini's
Restaurant in Beverly Hills with
Barbara Rush and Ronald Reagan.
Reagan was a former Democrat
moving toward the political right;
ten years later, Sinatra would
follow him.

In the first two or three decades of this century, Tin Pan Alley songs of this type were preceded by introductory verses. But by the Fifties verses were usually omitted in performance, recording and even, as here, composition. "One for My Baby" hardly eschews the conversational directness verses were meant to provide, however; the entire song is suffused with such naturalness. The very structure of its choruses incorporates miniature verses and refrains within each A section, offering eleven verselike bars before each mini-"chorus," which consists of the three-bar statement of the title and subtitle. What makes this less schematic than it sounds is the subtly conversational nature of the melodic line itself, the way it mirrors speech like an operatic recitative, rarely breaking into a real "tune" except in the "chorus" refrain.

This subtlety is echoed by the song's melodic and harmonic language. The vocal line is bluesily chromatic, adding and dropping sharps and flats at will and suggesting thereby the protagonist's unstable, disturbed state of mind. The first section in the sheet music is in E flat major, rising in tension and pitch to the key of G for the final ABA sections. The impression is of "through-composed" form—a seemingly uninterrupted meandering of narration, hesitant and heartbroken. The narrator's late-evening disorientation and despair are conveyed by choppy phrases, unsteady alternations between major and minor (those flatted blues thirds) and the refusal to return to the key in which the song began. A conventional song, based on normal practice in tonal classical music, will return by the end to the original key for symmetry's sake. To do otherwise carries with it dramatic connotations, in this case intimating the singer's inconclusiveness and confusion.

Narrative songs, amounting to miniature operatic vignettes, had been common in American popular music around the turn of the century (hence the greater popularity of verses then). But the narrative style, updated in language and musical idiom, suited Sinatra's dramatic instincts as well as his musical ones. This 1958 recording—singing, arrangement, production—is his greatest because it most completely calls upon his skills as both singer and actor.

The performance begins with a bluesy piano solo by Miller, who is placed at a distance—an effect heard best in stereo, and proof that even this early in stereo's development, when most pop producers contented themselves with vulgar Ping-Pong gimmicks, Cavanaugh was using the medium for dramatic purposes. Sinatra, by contrast, is front and center, as if he is hearing the piano from afar and we are right next to him, eavesdropping. His singing is full of the subtlest touches—recurrent appoggiaturas, or delicate little slurs from above the main note, and a near-classic use of rubato. *Tempo rubato* means "robbed time" in Italian. A soloist (or conductor, with the orchestra as his instrument) varies the flow of the music for expressive purposes, the variations set against the more regular metrical backdrop established in the listener's ear. Here, Riddle's arrangement creates a pulse, and then Sinatra prolongs phrases or bunches short notes together for purposes that are at once musical and dramatic: the lingering pauses of "another nickel . . . in the machine," for instance, or in the refrain "one more . . . for the road."

He also changes words and occasionally notes from the sheet-music version, all to make the lyrics and the vocal line more personal and natural for his own linguistic idiom: replacing *easy* for *dreamy*—it was *pretty* in 1947—and sensuously stretching out the *ea* . . . . . His most consistent interpretive touch is a delicious downward glissando, or slide, on the first syllable of *baby*, from the flatted third to the tonic.

Popular singers are expected to transpose songs into the keys most comfortable for their voices but to retain the harmonic relationships within a given song. Thus, "One for My Baby" can begin in any key but must move up a major third after the first chorus. In 1947, Sinatra had sung the song in B flat, ascending to D; in 1958 and 1966, even though his voice had darkened, he raised it up a whole tone, to C and E. The transposition heightens the fragility of the singing even further by shifting the center of the song's range into his slightly unsure transitional area just above middle C; his voice catches affectingly, for instance, at the end of the first chorus on its downward slide from E flat to C on the word *baby*.

Just before the end of that first chorus, Riddle brings up soft strings under the voice, and for the final chorus he inserts a broken saxophone solo. Sinatra's singing rises to a pained, repressed intensity at the climax: "This torch that I've found, must be drowned or it soon might explode . . ." By now, all of his artistry of declamation and phrasing has been forgotten in the face of the sheer, aching vulnerability of his voice—that shake, that quiver creeping in all the way down to his depths.

The song ends with slightly melodramatic coda of Sinatra's invention, extending the composers' "that long, long road" into a musing on *long* and *so long*. The singer drifts off into the aural distance, leaving the silent bartender and his pianist alone by themselves in the bar.

IT WAS NO ACCIDENT that both "Angel Eyes" and "One for My Baby" were barroom songs. Sinatra, the self-described "saloon singer"—who wasn't above using the first lines of "One for My Baby" ("So, set 'em up, Joe") as the lead-in to a Budweiser commercial in his 1965 television special—was the archetypal balladeer of what might be called the "booze sensibility," as compared with subsequent pop music and jazz fueled by heroin, marijuana, amphetamines, downers or cocaine. Not that he was ever an alcoholic. But a pugnacious macho lifestyle, mixed with a sometimes effusive emotionality, would have been unthinkable without neighborhood bars and their inflations all the way up to the Las Vegas casino, and was inseparable from Sinatra's personality. The late Fifties and Sixties saw him slipping back into another of those troughs in which his public image grew tacky and even sordid. This time, his commercial decline didn't approach the depths he reached in the early Fifties. But his pride in classiness and respect, attributes he treasured above all others, was at its lowest ebb.

Sinatra's apparently irresistible instinct to become embroiled in public fistfights, by himself or with his entourage of friends and bodyguards, had been a staple of the tabloids since the Forties and continued almost unabated, with one new, luridly publicized incident after another, well into the Seventies. While some were undoubtedly provoked, or in a just cause, there were numerous scraps in which the provoking party was at best in question, as in one ugly brawl in 1966 involving Sinatra, his principal hanger-on/bodyguard of the time, Jilly Rizzo, and a fifty-four-year-old businessman named Frederick R. Weisman, which took place in the Polo Lounge of the Beverly Hills Hotel. Sometimes these rows were overtly instigated by a cantankerous Sinatra. Gay Talese reports an incident in his 1966 *Esquire* article in which Sinatra almost came to blows in a private California club just because he took issue with the informal way that a younger man was dressed—and, by implication, with the younger generation's taste in fashion, music and lifestyles.

There can be little doubt, even after all due respect is paid to Sinatra's artistry

Conducting the fifty-six-piece Nelson Riddle Orchestra. Riddle, at center, was Sinatra's greatest arranger, who would define his sound throughout the 1950s, softening and refining the jazzish songs and underpinning the slower numbers with a subtle rhythmic impetus; for Arnold Shaw, Riddle was the key to Sinatra's "swinging ballad" style. His longtime producer Voyle Gilmore stands at far right

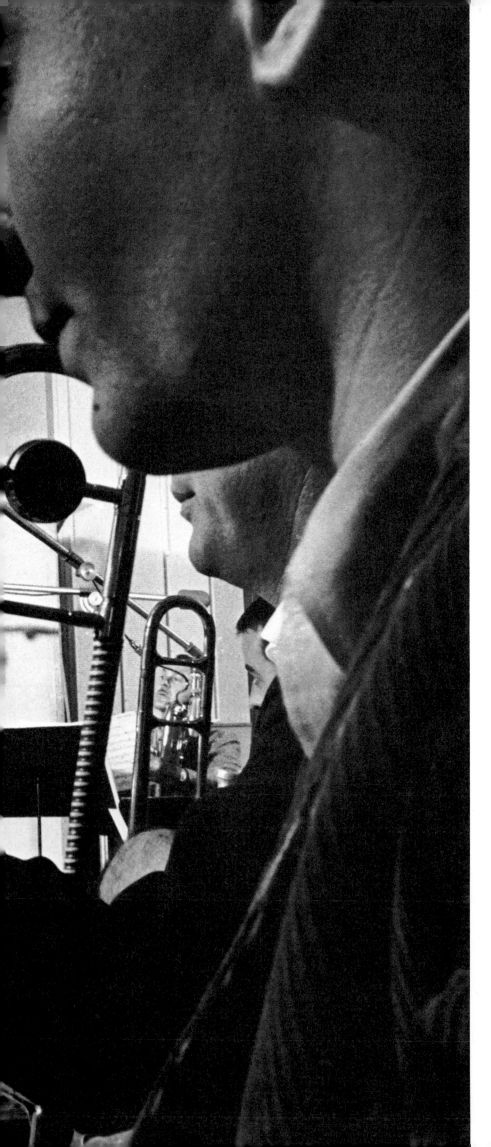

Previous page: A portrait of the
singer late in the 1950s. Left:
Entering the studio. All his life
Sinatra's mission has been to
preserve, to protect and to
enliven the great Tin Pan Alley
songs of the 1920s, 1930s, and
1940s. Next page: A recording
session with the Riddle orchestra.
The arranger created the style,
but Sinatra always maintained a
single-minded dominance over his
own work. By mid-decade, the LP
was challenging the single as the
preferred medium for pop music
recording; the critic Stephen
Holden has argued that Sinatra
pioneered the concept album.

and his undeniable good qualities, that he has a mean streak—especially when you consider his public humiliations of both men and women and his onstage vendettas against his enemies in the press, which became a fixture of his stage shows after the late Sixties. Even so loyal a friend as Sammy Davis, Jr., was once moved to comment on Sinatra's spitefulness—an indiscretion that led to his banishment from the inner circle for several anxious months. "I love Frank," he said on a 1960 radio show, "but there are many things he does that there is no excuse for. I don't care if you are the most talented man in the world. It does not give you the right to step on people and treat them rotten."

That said, it is probably difficult for anyone who has not observed the celebrity/tabloid press syndrome in full cry to realize what a bizarre public life a modern-day superstar must lead. We seem today to demand that our celebrities be rapidly built up and then viciously deflated, as if every instance of fame has to be punished by an equal measure of humiliation. The press can really be hysterical and parasitic, and some members of the public seem to ape its intrusiveness.

Often the motivation is not hostility, but sheer uncontrolled adoration. "I knew Elvis very well," commented Steve Wynn, the owner of the Golden Nugget casino in Atlantic City, in a 1983 *Philadelphia* magazine article. *"That's* what it's like. Crazy. People go berserk. Nice, well-dressed people. They come up, push you out of the way and then grab at him. I'm talking about irrational behavior. Sinatra needs security. It's the sickest thing I ever saw."

Elvis, of course, had a collection of goons and sycophants who went with him everywhere, cutting him off from the world far more completely than Sinatra allows himself to be. Sinatra is by nature a public man, accustomed to eating in restaurants, gambling in casinos, showing up at openings. When you add to that his reputation for feistiness and the predilection of some fans to test that reputation out of the same macho-barroom code that *he* grew up with, you have an explanation for many of his public confrontations.

Sinatra has been condemned for his irascibility and rambunctiousness when, say, the Who could not only run amok but win the approval of *their* generation for doing so. Rock stars drink and attract groupies and get into fights and break up hotels and devour the land like locusts, and it's dismissed as part of the rock & roll lifestyle. But such loutishness is not part of the ethos of Sinatra's generation—or, more precisely, their code of etiquette instructs them to deny that aspect of their own behavior.

Like Elvis, Sinatra always had an entourage. Back in the Forties it was called the Varsity. Then there was the Rat Pack, which grew out of Humphrey Bogart's circle in the mid-Fifties even if Sinatra was elected president. The Rat Pack was the source of the infamous Clan, which flourished in the late Fifties and early Sixties, and carries on in modified form to this day.

Its key members were Sinatra as leader, plus Dean Martin, Sammy Davis, Jr., Joey Bishop and, for a while, Peter Lawford. Unlike the more private Rat Pack, the Clan was prone to public cutups, performing together onstage in Las Vegas in their own shows or, sometimes, in others', as Eddie Fisher once discovered to his chagrin, when the Clan took over one of his casino openings, climbing up onstage from their ringside tables and joking and cavorting while Fisher stood there dumbfounded.

Clan activity also spilled into its film vehicles. While these movies made money, they accelerated the process of decline that had infected Sinatra's films and his attitude toward film as a place for serious work. They also soured public opinion on Sinatra, with their spectacle of middle-aged men struggling to

Leaving a Capitol recording session at three o'clock in the morning. The flip side of the singer's swaggering bravado was a poignant loneliness.

171

prolong the illusion of youth during a time when a *real* youth culture was taking shape before everyone's eyes. This sense of alienation from young people was heightened by Sinatra's increasingly ornate hep-cat slang—*bag, bird, broad*, etc. I can still recall my own feelings of generational hostility to finger-snapping, too-cool-for-words jazzish hipsters. This attitude is nowhere better displayed than in the title and contents of Sinatra's first album for his own Reprise label in 1961, *Ring-a-Ding-Ding*.

Sinatra's manic intensity at work and play contributed to the aura of desperation in the Clan's cavortings; the intensity derived, some said, from his deep-seated fear of another failure like the one that cut him down in the late Forties. The strain, combined with his closeness to the Clan, led to the painful termination of several close, longstanding friendships in 1963—nothing lurid or worthy of the tabloids, perhaps, but indicative of the crumbling of some of Sinatra's old values and ties. That year also brought the trauma of the kidnapping of his son, Frank, Jr., who was finally returned unharmed and the $240,000 ransom recovered. But then Sinatra had to endure defense allegations that the entire affair had been staged by his son to bolster his fledgling career as a singer. The kidnappers were eventually convicted, but an embarrassing doubt had been planted in the public's mind.

If Sinatra had been a womanizer since the early years of his first marriage, this period of rootless bachelorhood brought his sexual and romantic restlessness to a peak. He was briefly engaged to the dancer Juliet Prowse in 1962, but otherwise conducted an endless round of affairs and adventures. The actress Jill St. John was one name bandied about in the press, but many of Sinatra's playmates were, again, more anonymous, part of the Clan revels.

Some of those revels included a woman named Judith Campbell, and she led to new, even more dangerous allegations of mob involvement. Campbell (now known as Judith Campbell Exner) was by her own account a Sinatra girlfriend whom he introduced first to President Kennedy and shortly thereafter to the mobster Sam "Momo" Giancana, who had simultaneous affairs with her. It was about this time that the CIA allegedly made a contract with Giancana to assassinate Fidel Castro. The closest Sinatra came to commenting on any of this was when Campbell claimed she had broken off their relationship because his sexual tastes proved kinkier than hers. "Hell hath no fury like a hustler with a literary agent," he responded through his publicity spokesman.

Mafia rumors have dogged Sinatra all his life, from the Lucky Luciano incident in 1947, to rumors of Giancana meetings and business deals in the early Sixties that led to the uncontested denial of his Nevada gaming license in 1963, to his involvement in the Seventies with the mob-backed Westchester Premier Theater in New York and with a dog track about the same time. Sinatra has never been indicted or convicted, lives under the legal presumption of innocence and was named national chairman of the Italian American Anti-Defamation League in 1967. It is tempting to conclude that many of the Sinatra–Mafia rumors have capitalized on the sheer Italianness of his socializing, a form of warm bravado that can seem positively exotic to a non-Italian. Gay Talese has shown a special sympathy for the bonds that link Sinatra with his friends, associates and cronies, an Italian ethnicity similar to, but by no means identical with, the social world of the Mafia.

But Sinatra has had more tangible reasons to associate with figures with a shadowy connection to the underworld—without involving any unlawful behavior on his part. As a "saloon singer," he has to show common courtesy to the men

Left: Sinatra was still a staunch
liberal at the beginning of the
1960s. Eleanor Roosevelt
appeared on his 1960 television
special "Here's to the Ladies"
—and even joined him in a song.
Right: At a performance in Los
Angeles during the campaign
to elect Jack Kennedy.

After his victory, Kennedy
asked Sinatra to organize his
Inaugural Gala. Sharing in the
preparations are, from left: Gene
Kelly, Sinatra, Peter Lawford,
Nat "King" Cole, Janet Leigh, Tony
Curtis, Sammy Cahn, Governor
Edmund G. Brown of California
and Milton Berle. At the piano is
Jimmy Van Heusen. Next page:
With his friend Peter Lawford,
the president's brother-in-law.

who "run the saloons," as one Sinatra defender put it. Casino owners, in turn, whether or not they are skimming profits or laundering illicit cash, value his presence out of simple celebrity fascination, but also for his ability to attract customers. And thus they may seek to encourage his loyalty by offering him part ownership.

Whatever the whites, blacks and grays may have been in this complex relationship of Sinatra, casino owners and known mobsters, all the Mafia stories in the late Fifties seriously compromised his already tarnished image. His omnipresence on movie screens, records and the radio, the spate of stories about his boozing and carousing, and the Mafia investigations and insinuations combined to sour a relationship he held in special esteem.

Sinatra had continued his support for the Democrats and for liberal causes after Roosevelt's death in 1945. Perhaps his noblest moment had been his attempt in 1960 to hire the blacklisted screenwriter Albert Maltz, who had worked on Sinatra's 1945 short tolerance film, *The House I Live In.* Eventually, however, Sinatra capitulated to right-wing pressure—John Wayne was an outspoken Hollywood opponent—for fear that his crusade might jeopardize John F. Kennedy's chances for the Democratic presidential nomination.

With the Kennedys, Sinatra felt a real kinship—or at least he did with Jack Kennedy. He had met the senator through Peter Lawford and felt drawn to him as a young and vital figure, as a liberal Democrat, as a Catholic and as a fellow womanizer. Their closeness culminated in Sinatra's being asked to organize and star in Kennedy's Inaugural Gala in January 1961. But thereafter the friendship cooled, partly because Jackie apparently disapproved of the loose sex that came along with her husband's involvement with the Clan. More crucially, Bobby Kennedy—whom Gay Talese contends Sinatra and his circle resented as "an Irish cop, more dignified than those in Dolly's day, but no less intimidating"—was, in his capacity as the newly appointed attorney general, in hot pursuit of organized crime; he passed the word to his brother that Sinatra's associations in that world, or even the suspicion of such associations, made him a dangerous acquaintance. After Sinatra built a special wing at his Palm Springs home to receive a presidential visit in 1962, Jack Kennedy at the last moment chose to stay instead with Bing Crosby. It was a snub that Sinatra never forgot.

But Sinatra has never been one to let a personal disappointment impede his activity, on any front. Frustrated at others' ownership of his creative projects and no longer able to channel his energies into political fundraising, he spent the early Sixties steadily expanding his business empire, seeking control over all the projects he was associated with—a process that encompassed the establishment of his own record label, the production and direction of films, the part ownership of casinos and, at one point, the founding of his own talent agency (that sideline eventually fell through). Estimates of Sinatra's wealth, then as now, are impossibly vague. Earl Wilson, who was happy to print most anything, claimed Sinatra was worth $50 million in 1976, counting his additional investments in such nonentertainment fields as real estate, missile parts and aviation. Yet Arnold Shaw suggested that, in the early Sixties, Sinatra was grossing $20 million *annually*.

The most dramatic of these business moves was the founding in 1960 of his own record company, Reprise. This was to be Sinatra's haven from the philistinism and trendiness he perceived elsewhere in the record business, a place where he and artists he admired could record what they wanted the way they wanted.

With Reprise in the works, Sinatra's recording activity with Capitol declined at the end of the Fifties, even though, for contractual reasons, some Capitol sessions postdated his first Reprise sessions (including one final Stordahl album for Capitol, *Point of No Return*). That hardly meant a diminution in Sinatra releases. He had an inclination to overrecord, anyway, pouring out several albums a year like a country singer and thus risking overexposure. But in the early Sixties, a Sinatra war broke out between Reprise and Capitol, which flooded the market with releases, rereleases and budget releases in the hope of overpowering Sinatra's fledgling enterprise. The immediate result was millions of Sinatra records purchased, on both labels. Still, in 1963, Sinatra sold Reprise to Warner Bros., getting a one-third interest in return as well as guarantees of artistic autonomy and a piece of Warner's film action.

All this business activity, combined with his social life and political concerns, has led some critics to denigrate the Reprise albums of the Sixties, dismissing them as either tired rehashes of his Capitol style or, worse, unsure experimentation in the vain hope of recapturing the youth market. Neither charge holds up upon examination of the actual records. In fact, before he got desperate later in the decade, the artistic autonomy Sinatra enjoyed at Reprise inspired some of his most exciting experimentation. These explorations of idiom and style in the early to mid-Sixties were not a product of commercial insecurity but a logical extension of his earlier artistic inclinations.

More than anything else, that meant a more intense involvement with jazz. Some of Sinatra's first Reprise sessions involved Sy Oliver, the old Dorsey arranger, and resulted in an affectionate tribute album to his old boss, *I Remember Tommy*. After that, Sinatra extended his collaborations still further into jazz, with three Count Basie albums, none quite as memorable as might have been hoped but honorable, nonetheless. The collaboration with Duke Ellington, *Francis A. & Edward K.*, proved more appealing, with Billy May's arrangements neatly meshing Sinatra's singing with the mellow accompaniment of Ellington, his piano and his orchestra.

A related and highly successful musical exploration was Sinatra's collaboration with the Brazilian bossa nova musician Antonio Carlos Jobim. This was, in part, a commercial ploy, perhaps, since bossa nova had already made an impact not only on jazz, with Charlie Byrd and Stan Getz, but on the pop charts, with the Getz–Astrud Gilberto "Girl from Ipanema," a Top Five single in 1964 cowritten by Jobim. The Sinatra–Jobim pairing, which appeared on the *Francis Albert Sinatra & Antonio Carlos Jobim* album of 1967 and on one side of Sinatra's last pre-"retirement" album of 1971, *Sinatra & Company*, blended the singer's conversational vocals with the soft patter of Jobim's music to surprisingly apt effect.

There were also stillborn recording projects with Ella Fitzgerald and Oscar Peterson. In 1965, Sinatra embarked on a tour with the Basie band that included the Newport Jazz Festival. Since then, he has performed often with such jazz veterans as Fitzgerald and Sarah Vaughan. And he continued to use jazz sidemen in his studio sessions, musicians like Ben Webster and Juan Tizol who didn't ordinarily indulge in pop work.

None of which makes him a "real" jazz singer, in the sense of an improviser who lets his interaction with jazz instrumentalists spontaneously spark his creativity: Certainly, he never considered himself one. In the mid-Sixties, most jazz critics dismissed his apparent jazz pretensions; Whitney Balliett was especially derogatory about Sinatra's 1965 Newport appearance, suggesting that he had transformed Basie into a pop sideman for the duration of his perfunctory onstage stint.

In the 1960 film *Can-Can*, Juliet Prowse, as the dancer Claudine, offers her ankle to Sinatra, as the lawyer François Durnais. Fo a brief time in 1962, they would be engaged to be married.

Left: With Juliet Prowse at a
Hollywood costume party. Right:
During an early recording session
for Sinatra's own label, Reprise,
with Prowse, Sammy Cahn and,
seated, Sinatra's concertmaster
and occasional conductor Felix
Slatkin. Reprise was founded in
1960 and sold to Warner Bros.
only three years later.

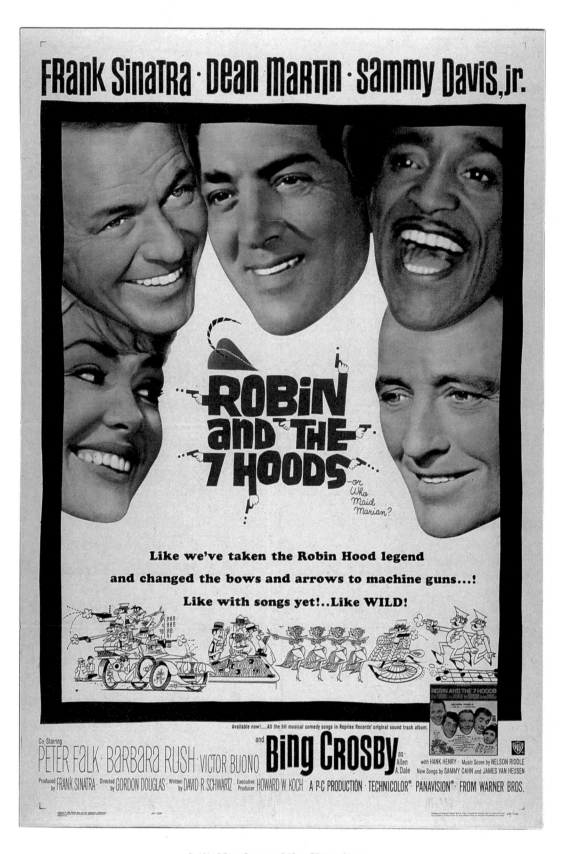

Left: Members of the Clan often shared stage and screen billings. In *Robin and the Seven Hoods* (1964), the Clan played madcap Chicago gangsters under the leadership of a swinging modern-day Robin Hood. Right: With Dean Martin, Peter Lawford and Sammy Davis, Jr., in another Clan vehicle, *Sergeants Three*, a comic remake of the classic *Gunga Din*.

Sinatra and Sammy Davis, Jr.,
in the early 1960s. Ten years
younger than Sinatra, Davis has
sometimes referred to him as
"my leader."

189

But Sinatra won the respect of many jazz musicians, who saw in him a kindred spirit. "Really, my man is Frank Sinatra," said Lester Young. In 1965, a poll of jazz musicians conducted by Leonard Feather named Sinatra "greatest ever" male vocalist. Sinatra got fifty-six votes, followed by Nat "King" Cole with thirteen, Billy Eckstine with eleven and Louis Armstrong with nine. By 1974, even Balliett had come around to the conclusion that Sinatra had, by sheer effort, turned himself into a genuine jazz singer.

Rigid categorization clouds the genuine affinities between his kind of pop and the jazz of the swing era. Sinatra's jazz inflections, as they emerged in the Fifties and Sixties, were born of powerful influences—Mercer, Holiday, James, Dorsey. Over the years, he became more flexible, more rhythmically alert and more percussively insistent in his phrasing of uptempo songs. And often his ballad singing, steady and measured despite its sinuous inflections, provided a wonderful, calm counterpoint to the fluent improvisations of the jazz instrumentalists who accompanied him (Sinatra used to insist that Harry "Sweets" Edison, the trumpeter, be given a separate microphone to work with).

Ultimately, Sinatra's style is best seen as a refinement and extension of a pop sensibility. He is a classically derived pop singer with ever more overt jazz influences—in the crucial sense that he prefers a secure framework within which to work, rehearsed and perfected in his mind. That fixed, notated exactitude extends far more pervasively into the arrangements and note choices of his singing than the loose understanding of a song's "chord changes" need do for an improvisatory jazz musician. Classical composers usually resist free, unstructured improvisation because they fear that spontaneous creativity encourages a regression into habit and mannerism. Sinatra seems to feel the same way.

Sinatra's recordings during the Sixties hardly eschewed the standard Tin Pan Alley ballad and uptempo collections that had defined his style and commercial success in the Fifties. During the first couple of years of Reprise, Riddle was still contractually bound to Capitol. For his standards albums, Sinatra turned more to Jenkins and a new man, Don Costa. The first Costa album, *Sinatra and Strings*, includes a version of the first song Sinatra sang as a new member of the Hit Parade in January 1943, Cole Porter's "Night and Day." This is one of the few songs he recorded four times—with Stordahl in his first solo session in 1942, with Riddle in 1956, with Costa in 1961 and with Joe Beck in 1977. The Costa version is without question the best of the lot. In 1942 the singing is sweet, light and immature. Riddle's version is one of his "swinging ballads," charming enough but inconsequential next to the lush, brooding romanticism of the Costa arrangement. Here the tempo is slower than before, and for the only time on records Sinatra sings the introductory verse. (About the 1977 disco version, blessedly released only as a U.S. single and in Italy, the less said the better.)

Better still were a series of retrospective, autumnal albums of the mid- to late Sixties, the parallel to his Fifties ballad albums but suffused now with a regret and even remorse all the more poignant for being surrounded by an exuberant youth culture. *Cycles*, from 1968, is one of those albums, and the title track of the next year's *My Way*, most often remembered for its surging climaxes, is actually more an introspective reflection ("And now, the end is near . . ."). The best of these was the Jenkins-arranged *September of My Years*, which won the album of the year Grammy for 1965. It included a wonderfully wistful "Hello Young Lovers," a touching "September Song" and "It Was a Very Good Year," which Stephen Holden has called "an exceptionally eloquent expression of middle-aged erotic nostalgia."

greatest singer to emerge from the Tin Pan Alley tradition condemned 1950s rock & roll as "sung, played and written for the most part by cretinous goons." But on ABC's "Frank Sinatra Timex Show," he formally welcomed Elvis Presley home from the army. By the mid-1960s, it became almost impossible for singers like Sinatra to make the rock-dominated charts.

But Sinatra's repertory and arrangements did indeed turn desperate in the late Sixties and Seventies, *desperate* meaning impelled more by a desire to retain or regain commercial success than by any pure artistic impulse. His most pitiful efforts to extend his idiom—pitiful in the sense that they clashed egregiously with his style—came as he struggled to adapt to the rock and folk-rock music, and to the youth-oriented marketing policies, that dominated the record business from the late Sixties on.

Up until then, or at least until the British Invasion of 1964, defenders of the Tin Pan Alley faith had reasonable grounds to hope that eventually the rock fad would pass and "their" music would reassert itself. Rock lovers tend to think of American pop-music history as split between pre- and post-1955, with Elvis dividing the seas like Moses and the pop charts dominated forevermore by rock & roll. It just wasn't so. Sinatra, as we have seen, enjoyed his most commercially dominant period in the mid- to late Fifties, simultaneously with such unregenerate rock & rollers as Doris Day, Dean Martin, Vic Damone, Debbie Reynolds and Perry Como. By the late Fifties, with Presley, Jerry Lee Lewis, Chuck Berry and Buddy Holly out of action in one way or another, rock's energy seemed to be abating. Johnny Mathis was a big star, Percy Faith had the Number One single of 1960, Ferrante and Teicher and Lawrence Welk were big sellers in 1961 and the Singing Nun's "Dominique" topped the singles chart for a while in 1963.

After the mid-Sixties, however, it became almost impossible for singers like Sinatra to make the charts, so thoroughly dominated were they by British rock bands and their American counterparts. This is widely presumed among rock fans to represent the triumph of good over evil, and so it may have been. But for such Tin Pan Alley polemicists as Sidney Zion, it was the result of the record companies' faddish, shortsighted concentration on the youth market and youth music.

Sinatra himself had been fiercely scornful of rock & roll in the Fifties, an attitude tied up with the ASCAP–BMI battle. His 1961 album *Ring-a-Ding-Ding* came complete with liner notes by the critic Ralph J. Gleason, who had not yet embraced rock & roll as he would do so fervently just a few years later. His notes, which clearly reflected Sinatra's own feelings and were intended as a proclamation of policy for the new Reprise label, began: "In the midst of some of the aural horrors that roar out of the radio and the juke boxes these days . . ." Earlier, Sinatra had referred derisively to such "masterpieces as 'Hound Dog' and 'Be-Bop-a-Lula,' " and later noted that "rock 'n' roll fosters almost totally negative and destructive reactions in young people." Rock music was, he added, "sung, played and written for the most part by cretinous goons. My only deep sorrow is the unrelenting insistence of recording and motion-picture companies upon purveying this most brutal, ugly, degenerate, vicious form of expression." On other occasions, he had called rock "a rancid-smelling aphrodisiac" and "the martial music of every sideburned delinquent."

Such feelings, which he claimed to have modified in later years, didn't stop him from trying his hand at rock. He had timidly tested the waters with a quasi-rock arrangement in 1955 with Dave Cavanaugh, and had "welcomed" Presley back from the Army in a 1960 television special, treating Elvis in a "condescending" manner, according to the *Reporter*.

By the Sixties, however, Sinatra began adapting various soft-rock composers into his repertory, with songs between then and now by the likes of Jim Croce, Jimmy Webb, Neil Sedaka, John Denver, Paul Simon, Joni Mitchell, Stevie Wonder, Peter Allen, Billy Joel and various Beatles, not to speak of such peddlers

With the young Quincy Jones in 1964, discussing a Reprise recording of "It Might As Well Be Swing," arranged by Sy Oliver and featuring Count Basie. Two decades later, Jones produced Sinatra's *L.A. Is My Lady*.

Sinatra and Basie toured together in 1965, recording their live concerts at the Sands in Las Vegas in January 1966. Some critics charged that Sinatra had reduced Basie's orchestra to a backup band.

Left: Sinatra cutting his third
wedding cake in 1966 with
twenty-year-old Mia Farrow.
Right: On a boat with Farrow in
Hyannisport, Massachusetts. The
marriage seemed doomed to
failure on generational grounds;
by late 1967 they had separated
and by 1968 were divorced.

of middle-of-the-road rockoid bombast as Neil Diamond and Barry Manilow. There was even talk of an LP to be produced by George Harrison. Most of the rock songs Sinatra recorded came out dreadfully, with stiff vocal phrasing and, worse, hopelessly anachronistic instrumental arrangements. He also essayed soft-rock concept albums, with an incongruous collection of wispy Rod McKuen musings, *A Man Alone*, and a more persuasive suite entitled *Watertown*, by Bob Gaudio and Jake Holmes.

His most successful forays into the youth market came within his own family. In 1967 he joined his daughter Nancy in a duet, "Somethin' Stupid," that rose to Number One on the charts and won him his first gold single. Nancy enjoyed something of a run in 1965–66 with three Top Ten singles of her own, including the catchy Number One "These Boots Are Made for Walking."

Extramusically, Sinatra surprised everyone, his inner circle included, by marrying the twenty-one-year-old Mia Farrow in 1966. The marriage seemed doomed from the start, on generational grounds more than simple age differences. Farrow could never accept the rude humor and male-bonding machismo of the Sinatra circle: "All they know how to do is tell dirty stories, break furniture, pinch waitresses' asses and bet on the horses," she complained. When she drifted off to India with the Beatles to commune with the Maharishi, the marriage was on the way out; they were separated in late 1967 and divorced in 1968.

One might have thought that the softer folk-rock style of the early Seventies, with such writers as John Denver, James Taylor and the mature Carole King, as well as the solo Paul Simon and Randy Newman, would have been a new source of sophisticated adult material for Sinatra; certainly most of these singer-songwriters were resisted by rock purists as subverters of the rock spirit. Similarly, Sinatra might have sought to adapt his idiom to country pop, which in sociological terms would have represented a logical extension of his audience. Willie Nelson, after all, has recently crossed back to Tin Pan Alley with some success.

But country music, even the urbanized Nashville brand, was too distant from Hoboken and New York. Sinatra did appear in joint casino engagements with Denver in the mid-Seventies. But by then he had apparently lost the requisite flexibility, as the pitiful 1977 disco "Night and Day" suggests all too well. ("All or Nothing at All" and "Sorry Is the Hardest Word" were also taped at the same Joe Beck session, but neither has been released in any form.) Or, more likely, he never had a hope of adapting to the new: The image of this apostle of tough-guy swingerdom struggling with the girlish hippie wonder of Joni Mitchell's "From Both Sides Now" on his *Cycles* album, recorded in 1968, is about as convincing as Sid Vicious and "My Way." Even when Sinatra's vocals retained a plausible contemporaneity, his commitment to the sound of a studio orchestra, derived from the classical symphonic ensemble, dated his records in the age of the electric guitar.

Ultimately, though, his failure to adapt was a curious attestation to his strengths. Sinatra's distinction as a singer is his fidelity to his roots and to the style that he honed in the Fifties. In the Sixties, Seventies and even Eighties, he was still exploring and deepening that style. But a man so fervently identified with his own generation could hardly be expected singlehandedly to cross over to a young audience at the very height of the "generation gap." If singers such as Willie Nelson and Linda Ronstadt are now crossing back over from the opposite direction, it is not necessarily that they are more adaptable; the gap has begun to close by itself, and perhaps it is easier to look backward than forward.

By the end of the Sixties, things seemed bleak for Sinatra on every front. He could find no appropriate film scripts. He was disenchanted with the Democrats. His right hand (his microphone hand) was crippled with an arthritic condition, forcing his withdrawal from a 1970 Warner Bros. film. (The hand problem was eventually corrected by surgery.) There was an ugly confrontation at Caesars Palace in Las Vegas, with a casino official, Sanford Waterman, pulling a gun on him.

Worst of all, he couldn't find solace in his music, as he had always done before. Rock seemed triumphant, and he had enormous difficulty unearthing decent songs in his favored Tin Pan Alley tradition, quite apart from that tradition's loss of commercial viability. Sinatra's songwriter associates had run dry; they couldn't adapt to the new, and they found it increasingly difficult to be creative in an idiom the public rejected as dated. For Sinatra himself, it was becoming more and more incongruous to reach out beyond his stylistic circle to younger composers who might have enjoyed working with him. "There's a lot of garbage out there," he complained, clearly referring to more than just rock. "Nobody's writing any songs for me and I don't know what to do about it."

What he did was announce his retirement, complete with a gala farewell appearance at a benefit concert at the Dorothy Chandler Pavilion in Los Angeles on June 13, 1971. The occasion generated enormous emotion and numerous reflective articles about Sinatra, his career and how, as Pete Hamill put it, "in the past five years, Sinatra and his America began to drift apart."

BUT OF COURSE the retirement didn't, couldn't "take": Sinatra is too restless for that. It's not just that he craves the limelight, although that seems to be a part of it. He simply has to work, and without work, he becomes more agitated and nervous than ever.

The principal activity of his retirement years (1971–73) was his political shift from left to right. The move had been in the making since his snub by John Kennedy in 1962 and was sealed after further airings of his mob connections scuttled his participation in the Humphrey presidential campaign of 1968 (Sinatra had supported Humphrey in his California primary race against Robert Kennedy). By the late Sixties, he was playing golf with Vice-President Spiro Agnew, whose tough-guy denunciations of all and sundry he found refreshing. In 1970, he supported his old acquaintance Ronald Reagan in his reelection campaign for California governor. Even then, however, he gave signs of possibly siding with George McGovern and the Democrats in the 1972 presidential race, but eventually joined the Nixon camp and actively fundraised for the Republicans. From then on, he has been a firm Republican, supporting Gerald Ford and, especially, Ronald Reagan in his presidential race in 1980.

Sinatra's political odyssey has been greeted with everything from cynicism on the right to regret and overt hostility on the left. The most common sympathetic interpretation from the left was the sort expressed by Hamill, who saw in Sinatra's turn to Reagan a "disgust with the glib contempt of so many young, the resentment of a self-educated man" against campus protests and "a drift into a kind of natural conservatism that comes with age."

But for most left-wing writers and rock publications, his shift to Nixon and eventually to Reagan, his socializing with Republican fat cats, his opening of the Sun City casino in the South African "homeland" of Bophuthatswana in 1981, offered the image of a man both degenerate and cynically corrupt, with the last remnants of youthful innocence and liberal fervor long since burned away. That

A portrait of Sinatra in the late 1960s. During that time, the swinger seemed as archetypal as the wide-shouldered, bow-tied crooner of the 1940s and the gray-haired, tuxedo-clad Las Vegas star of the 1970s and 1980s

Sinatra would carry his tough, cynical image into his films, playing such roles as a hard-bitten, hard-loving, antihero private eye in the 1967 feature *Tony Rome*.

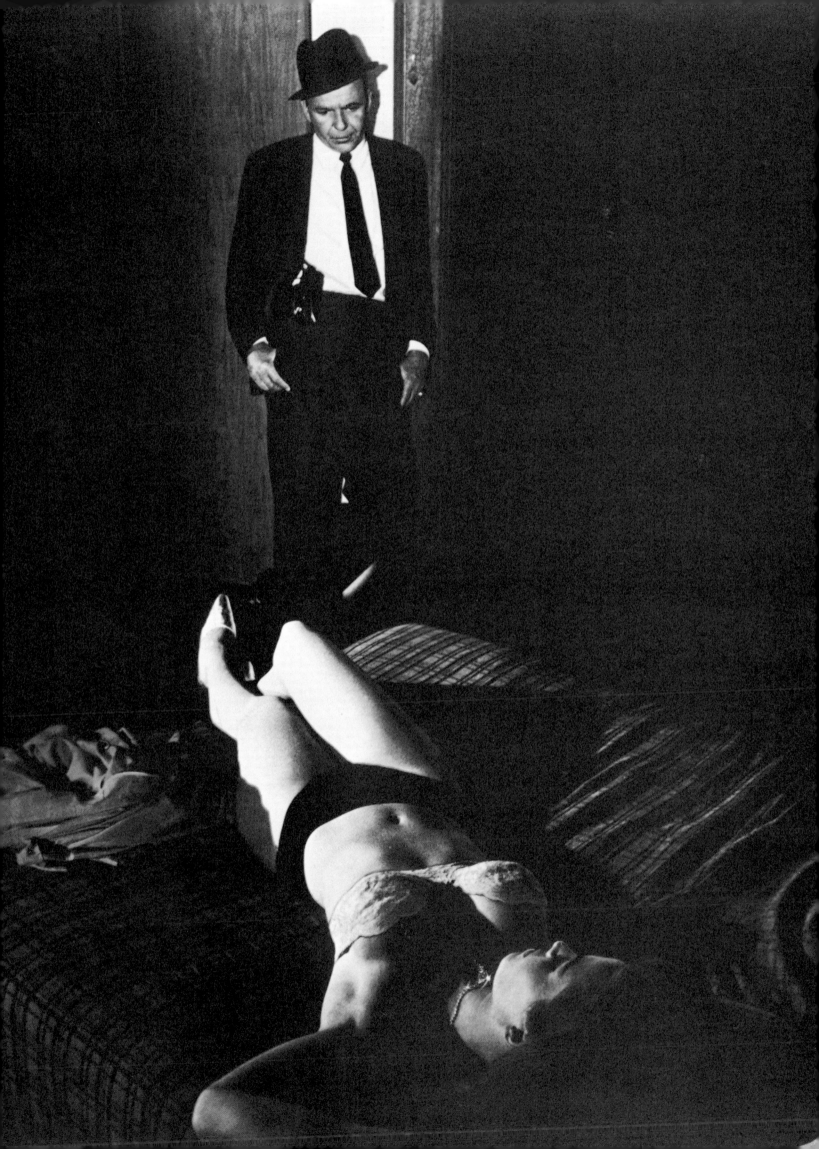

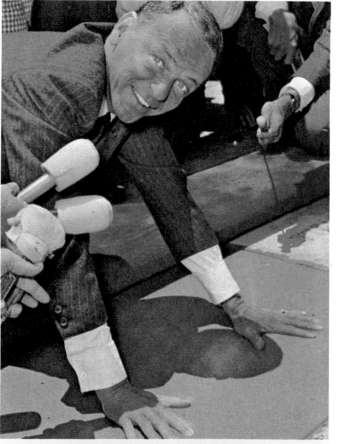

HANDPRINT CEREMONY-
GRAUMAN'S
CHINESE THEATRE

Left: In the recording studio with his daughter Nancy. Their 1967 duet, "Somethin' Stupid," went to Number One and, strangely enough, became Sinatra's first gold single. Right: Placing his hands in the wet cement at Grauman's Chinese Theater in Hollywood. "At this stage of my career," he told *Life* magazine, "I don't have any mountains left to climb."

Left: The funeral of Sinatra's father in January 1969. Right: That same month, at a dinner for the astronauts. By the end of the decade, things looked bleak for Sinatra on every front. Rumors linking him to the Mafia had scuttled his work for Humphrey's 1968 presidential campaign, and there were no suitable film roles forthcoming. But worst of all, "Nobody's writing songs for me," he said, "and I don't know what to do about it."

Sinatra may have had plausible reasons for supporting Reagan, or that he had continued his charitable work, including a benefit to support the search for the mass killer of black children in Atlanta only a few months before his South African engagement, meant little to his new set of ideological opponents. Throughout his life, Sinatra has aspired to be perceived as classy. For many, his elbow rubbing with Nixon, Reagan and company seemed the ultimate in tackiness.

Perhaps the most grieving of these moral denunciations came from Ralph J. Gleason in *Rolling Stone*. Writing in 1974, shortly before his death, this jazz partisan who had become a champion of rock and youth culture lashed out against what he saw as Sinatra's betrayal of ideals they had once shared.

"It is simply weird now to see him all glossed up like a wax dummy, with that rug on his head looking silly, and the onstage movement, which used to be panther-tense, now a self-conscious hoodlum bustle," Gleason wrote. "What seemed like a youthful bravado twenty-five years ago seems like angry perversity now. Ol' Blue Eyes is a drag that Frankie never was . . . I don't believe, anymore, that he is one of us. He's one of *them* now, singing from the other side of the street and I guess he doesn't even have a whiff of how power mad and totalitarian it all seems . . ."

But Gleason also said, in the same article, "He doesn't have to be a nice guy to be a great singer. And he *is* a great singer." Or, as Dave Marsh put it in *Elvis*: "Does the monstrosity of Elvis really matter? He remained a great artist, and the way he sang contains more 'truth' than all the demeaning facts that have festered since his death." Charles Aznavour carried that argument one step further. Speaking of Sinatra, he said, "It is impossible to sing like a saint and be a bad man."

Rock criticism has brought a welcome reassertion of humanistic values and moral urgency to music criticism. But sometimes moral confidence can grow self-righteously intolerant, and sometimes ethical concern can overwhelm art itself. Without reverting to a detached formalism, Marsh and Aznavour suggest that an artist's work may speak more truthfully about life and the artist than his or her own actions. And finally, who's to say, with absolute confidence, that Frank Sinatra has become an immoral man? There is plenty of evidence to support the contrary conclusion.

It is also possible to interpret Sinatra's shift to the right as ideologically coherent, even if one still regrets it. Like much of Middle America, Sinatra retains a fierce belief in the integrity of the "little man"; his populism, no less unprecedented in American history than that of Marxist leftists, stems from a Jacksonian faith in democracy and the ability of local organization to resist oppressive forces from without. In the Thirties, with his mother a Democrat and the country in the depths of a depression, those forces seemed to be big business and capitalism itself. In the Seventies, the villains had become big labor and, worst of all, big government, and Sinatra was ready for a reversion to the kind of Taft Republicanism that Reagan seemed to espouse. From Sinatra's point of view, his constant battles with state and federal officials over his alleged Mafia ties were proof of government malevolence.

In July 1972, shortly after being subpoenaed on Mafia matters by a congressional committee and just prior to his full-scale involvement in the Nixon campaign, Sinatra contributed an article to the *New York Times* Op-Ed page entitled "We Might Call This the Politics of Fantasy." "There are some larger questions raised by my appearance that have something to say to all of us," he wrote. "The most important is the rights of a private citizen in this country when faced with the huge machine of the central Government."

With his daughter Nancy at her wedding in Cathedral City, California, in December 1970. Four years later, Sinatra became a grandfather for the first time.

With fewer concert appearances to attract media attention during this period, Sinatra's charity activities and awards received greater coverage than ever, with groundbreaking ceremonies for the dedication of hospital wings he had funded, the reception of the Jean Hersholt Humanitarian Award at the 1971 Oscar ceremony, and a State of Israel Medallion of Valor award in 1972. The truth is, however, that Sinatra has always been active in charitable causes, from the most public to the anonymously private, paying the hospital bills and rent checks of entertainers and business associates who range from dear friends to bare acquaintances and showering them with lavish, unexpected gifts. This generosity has occasioned a good deal of derision, especially the stint of charity concerts Sinatra did in the early Sixties in an apparent effort to patch up his image after being dropped by the Kennedys. To this day, William Safire seems convinced that Sinatra's charitable activity, which by this time involves multimillion-dollar benefits with the likes of Diana Ross and Luciano Pavarotti, is a crass attempt by a barely disguised Mafioso to buy latter-day respectability.

Perhaps, but such cynicism may also mask a curious kind of Me Generation selfishness by accusers who aren't nearly as generous. Sinatra's charitable efforts are more likely, in Gay Talese's perceptive analysis, part of his self-image as a Sicilian *padrone*, one of the men who are called *uomini respettati* and are, in Talese's words, "both majestic and humble, men who are loved by all and are very generous by nature, men whose hands are kissed as they walk from village to village, men who would *personally* go out of their way to redress a wrong." For all his vendettas and pugnacious barroom behavior, Sinatra seems to be deeply loved by his peers, to judge from innumerable attestations and the quite remarkable effusions of admiration during the 1983 Variety Clubs International television special.

The suspicions about the genuineness of Sinatra's charitable concerns are mirrored in the assumption—partly correct, in this case—that his periodic milestone celebrations (the twenty-five years in show business special in 1965, the forty-year special in 1980, even his 1971 retirement and the comeback hoopla two years later) are careful ploys to keep himself in the public eye, career cards dealt with cool-eyed calculation. It has been less persuasively suggested that his brawls and public feuding with writers (most recently Maxine Cheshire, Rex Reed, Rona Barrett and Kitty Kelley) were part of preconceived publicity campaigns.

The Cheshire blowup was his most lurid yet. In 1973, at a pre-Inaugural party, he cussed out the *Washington Post* columnist, apparently in response to yet another Mafia rehash. "Get away from me, you scum," he cried. "Go home and take a bath. I'm getting out of here, to get rid of the stench of Mrs. Cheshire. You know Mrs. Cheshire, don't you? That stench you smell is from her. You're nothing but a two-dollar cunt. You know what that means, don't you? You've been laying down for two dollars all your life. Here's two dollars, baby, that's what you're used to." He then stuffed two dollar bills in her drink and stalked away.

With these press explosions—he repeated much of the Cheshire language in concerts for several months to come and then erupted with denunciations of the Australian press the following year—some of the cynicism may seem warranted. He certainly got a lot of publicity mileage out of the Australian fiasco. "I used to blow whole countries," he announced on his return. "Now I blow continents." These altercations were supposed to have caused his career irreparable damage at the time, or so said the press, always innocently convinced of the public's support. But in fact they seem to have redounded to his favor, bolstering his image as the

In the late 1960s and early 1970s Sinatra would look to the rock music he had scorned as a source of new material, even attempting an album with Rod McKuen. Finally, in 1971, he announced his retirement—but he would return to the limelight less than three years later.

Above: A self-described "saloon singer," Sinatra is the classic balladeer of what might be called the "booze sensibility." Right: Always a generous giver, Sinatra devoted more time than ever to charity work after he retired. In 1971, he played in the Los Angeles Police Department's Celebrity Golf Invitational to raise funds for underprivileged children.

After a White House dinner,
where Sinatra had performed in
April 1973. From the left are
Vice-President Spiro Agnew;
Prime Minister Guilio Andreotti
of Italy, with his wife; Sinatra;
First Lady Pat and President
Richard Nixon; and Judy Agnew.
Sinatra was so warmly received
by his audience that he began to
consider a comeback.

With Barbara Blakely, formerly married to Zeppo Marx, at a 1974 tribute to James Cagney. She would become Sinatra's wife in July 1976.

tough guy who lashes out against innuendo and scurrilous press attacks. The Cheshire imbroglio hurt him not at all with the Nixon administration, which had no love for the *Washington Post* and soon invited him and Perry Como to sing at the White House reception for the prime minister of Italy. Humphrey Bogart once said that "Sinatra's idea of paradise is a place where there are plenty of women and no newspapermen. He doesn't know it, but he'd be better off if it were the other way round." But it may well be that he does know it; certainly no one has better managed to sustain the interest of the press over a near-fifty-year span than he.

Whether or not he was a master manipulator, his carefully orchestrated comeback in late 1973—with a new motto and album to match, *Ol' Blue Eyes Is Back*, plus attendant television special, followed in 1974 by the Main Event tour and live album from Madison Square Garden—did not go smoothly. The comeback album was tepidly greeted, and its most appropriate new song, Stephen Sondheim's "Send in the Clowns," while beautifully done, paled commercially before the subsequent Judy Collins version. Some critics complained that his voice was gone (the *Toronto Globe and Mail* called him "a vocal has-been, ripping off those who care about his music rather than his personality"), and his television special finished third in a three-way ratings race. He wasn't even selling out in Las Vegas; two shows at top prices in January (traditionally a slow month, to be sure) drew only four hundred customers per night to the twelve-hundred-seat Caesars Palace.

But not all his concerts were poor, or poorly attended, and by the late Seventies, Sinatra's image had begun to shift back toward the positive. One reason was that he seemed to be settling down, assuming a more dignified, even opulent, image with which the newly affluent, rapidly aging Me Generation could identify. People had hoped before that Sinatra was settling down—in the early Sixties, in the early Seventies. But by the mid-Seventies events conspired to give him a real impetus to do so. One was the continued difficulties he faced finding suitable songs and film scripts. Another, quite simply, was age: As he edged into his sixties, it became increasingly difficult, or perhaps just unseemly, to sustain his frenetic pace and macho image. This sense of aging was brought home by the death of his beloved mother, Dolly, in a private-plane crash in 1977.

A more positive explanation for his new maturity was his marriage in 1976 to Barbara Blakely Marx, who had been living with him for several years and who had been previously married to Zeppo Marx. She was the kind of glamorous yet supportive wife he hadn't found in three previous efforts, a woman who understood his world (she was once a Las Vegas showgirl) and was willing to subordinate herself to him. Among other signs of that devotion was her conversion to Catholicism, to which Sinatra had returned with greater fervor than he had sometimes shown in the past.

After a desultory relationship with recording between 1974 and 1979—he did occasional sessions, but rejected almost everything—Sinatra reentered the studio in the summer of 1979 to make his three-disc statement, *Trilogy*. This anthology of "past, present and future" was not entirely successful; as with his life itself, his enemies might argue, the past was terrific, the present tolerable and the future embarrassing. But the singing throughout was remarkable, and the album as a whole, by its very blockbuster nature, attracted the attention not just of Tin Pan Alley loyalists but of rock and jazz critics, as well. The followup, *She Shot Me Down* (1981), won warm reviews both for its singing, which had taken on an endearing patina of age, and for the songs selected—especially another Sondheim number, "Good Thing Going," from the musical *Merrily We Roll Along*.

With Barbara and his eighty-two-year-old mother, Dolly, in Israel in 1976, when Sinatra received the Mount Scopus award for his charitable activities. Two months later, Dolly would die in an airplane crash on her way to one of her son's concerts.

In 1980, Sinatra made his first theatrical film in a decade, *The First Deadly Sin*, opposite Faye Dunaway. He continued his sumptuous round of charity concerts, often performing with opera stars (either an attestation of affinities or, more likely, a calculated choice to appeal to people who could afford benefit-ticket prices). In 1981 he organized the Reagan Inaugural Gala—Reagan's first, his second—which hardly won over the leftist cognoscenti but did reinforce his new, tuxedo-clad image. In 1983 came the massive, sixteen-disc audiophile Original Master Recordings box of his Capitol albums, which triggered a new flood of press attention, as well as the Twyla Tharp ballets and the laudatory television specials at the end of the year.

As if to reassert his traditional role in the public arena, Sinatra even managed to inflame his antagonism with the press, by announcing that he intended to sue the author Kitty Kelley on the spurious grounds that he had the rights to his own life story. This provoked horrified knee-jerk denunciations for his supposed assault on the First Amendment, thus garnering reams of publicity for both Kelley and Sinatra.

And he was still alive creatively, still testing the limits of his versatility, going into the recording studio in the spring of 1984 with his longtime, sometime collaborator Quincy Jones, who came fresh from his own triumphs with Michael Jackson. The resulting album, *L.A. Is My Lady*, was Sinatra's best record in years. Jones's production elegantly blended big-band verities with contemporary flavoring, and an all-star band (George Benson, the Brecker Brothers) buoyed up the singing. The song selection was at a high level, too, apart from the smarmy title track. There was a mixture of ballads and uptempo tunes, with the slower material once more enlivened by jazz and the fast songs refined by feeling. This was no mere celebration of fading superstardom. It was a vital musical statement by an artist seemingly eager to prove he had something to say to an audience doting on his imitators.

What was it that caused the present exaltation of the Sinatra reputation, his transmutation into the elder statesman of American popular culture? The answer would seem to be the evolution of his voice and style, but also a shift in the cultural and intellectual climate.

As a musician, he of course appeals to sentimentalists—both to those who were there during his youth or who made out to his torch albums of the Fifties and also to the new generation of camp and conservative nostalgists. But there is also much to admire in Sinatra's continued skill as a musician and in the way he has adapted his style to suit his declining powers.

Vocally, in his late sixties, Sinatra is a technical paragon. His singing has remained remarkably secure at an age when the typical opera singer has long since retired. Yes, his voice is grittier than ever, and a shortness of breath requires him not only to intersperse his singing during concerts with instrumental solos and separate band numbers but also to cultivate a choppier singing style. That means more percussively aggressive phrasing than ever; indeed, his entire shift from the smooth ballads of the Forties to increasingly jazzish uptempo songs can be explained in part on purely technical grounds. His new emphasis on jazz may also be seen in his recent decision to switch his concert arrangements to a more upbeat band sound. New, too, is his custom of reading the lyrics from a music stand.

But the voice remains essentially the same, a longevity that can only be explained by his natural ease of vocal production, compared with the more effortful projection of opera singers or such pop-rock belters as (in their different ways) Neil Diamond, Barry Manilow and Bruce Springsteen. Once again, as

On the 1976 Jerry Lewis Muscular Dystrophy Telethon, with his longtime close friend Dean Martin.

Rehearsing with Sarah Vaughan for a mid-1970s concert series at the London Palladium. Sinatra revered the great female jazz singers—Vaughan, Billie Holiday, Ella Fitzgerald—and performed with several of them in the course of his career. It was Mabel Mercer, he once claimed, who taught him to handle a lyric.

Left: By the late 1970s, Sinatra has become a revered elder statesman of American popular culture. Right: Singing for his favorite baseball team, the Dodgers. Sinatra's voice has remained remarkably secure over the years; he has recorded his recent albums at an age when most opera singers have retired.

well, Sinatra has found new ways to turn vocal insecurity into fragile expressiveness; the ballads on his recent albums, and particularly such Forties nostalgia arrangements as those accorded "It Had to Be You" and "More Than You Know" on *Trilogy*, attain a new poignancy from their very unsureness.

The first, "past" record in the *Trilogy* set affords an especially instructive field for comparison, since it contains several songs that Sinatra recorded at least once, and usually more often, in his own past. The Jerome Kern–Oscar Hammerstein II "Song Is You," for instance, is another of those Sinatra favorites he recorded four times; but unlike "Night and Day," with its final disco version, all four represent serious, creatively successful efforts on Sinatra's part. The four versions are from the first Axel Stordahl solo session in 1942, with Stordahl again in 1947, with Billy May in 1958 and, finally, with May again for *Trilogy* in 1979.

The four divide into two halves, two ballads with Stordahl and two swinging versions with May, yet all told, they represent a steady progression toward a more energetic idiom. The Stordahl versions are similar, but the first is blander and more sentimental than the second, with the 1942 version ascending to a cooing falsetto high F at the end. The May versions, conversely, drive jazzily forward, and if the 1958 recording ultimately seems the best statement of this approach, sweeter and more relaxed, the 1979 version reveals a confident, practiced authority appealing on its own terms.

Victor Young's "Street of Dreams" offers a more complex progression. In 1942, with the Dorsey band and the Pied Pipers, it was a literally dreamy ballad. In 1966, with Quincy Jones and the Basie band live at the Sands, it had become a driving swing tune, invigorating in its energy. For May in 1979, it was still swinging, but here the synthesis between ballad and big band comes only in Sinatra's full maturity, and this performance is clearly the preferable one of the three.

All these records can be discussed in terms of technique and phrasing. But what makes Sinatra so marvelous this late in life is his unflagging commitment to his craft and art. He never gave up, never (or hardly ever) let even the silliest material overcome his sense of style, never (for long, at least) allowed the routine of performance or the indulgences of vast wealth to dull his desire to do the very best he could. For Sinatra, a performance is nothing unless it is invested with emotion and excitement. He was angrily disappointed by one Frank, Jr., performance in 1963. "Don't ever let me catch you singing like that again, without enthusiasm," he told his son backstage. "You're nothing if you aren't excited by what you're doing." And in one of the most famous of all Sinatra quotations, to *Playboy* that same year: "You can be the most artistically perfect performer in the world, but the audience is like a broad—if you're indifferent, endsville."

It is not easy to sustain conviction amid the blandishments of celebrity adulation. "My Way" wasn't Elvis's song. But he used to sing it in his last years, anyway, and the concert performance captured from 1977 is a wreck: technically rough, bellowed and howled at the climaxes, wooden in feeling. The difference between the Sid Vicious and Elvis Presley versions of this song is the difference between intended and unintended embarrassment. Sinatra had just as much money as Elvis, just as many excuses to let himself slide. But he didn't; he survived, and he still gives it all he's got.

But that was a Sinatra constant. What changed by the late Seventies was the context in which he was perceived. It wasn't just the nationwide drift to the political right. All the arts seem to be shifting from the more rigorous tenets of modernism toward a new openness, accessibility and eclecticism—from the new concern for narration in fiction, to realism in painting, to the historically minded stylistic diversity of the new jazz, to the "new romanticism" in contemporary classical music. And it is certainly perceptible in pop music. In 1977, there were nine radio stations in the major markets playing nothing but Tin Pan Alley standards; in 1984, there were one hundred seventy-three. Even such punkish bands as the Lounge Lizards took to wearing Sinatra-style skinny ties and snap-brim hats. Nostalgia had become a fashion in itself, with new bands recycling idioms from every era of pop.

Rock today seems at bleaker moments to be divided between schlock and shock, a few obvious superstars aside—trendy techno-pop, tired rock and middle-of-the-road recyclings on the one hand, punk and street funk on the other. Left out is that broad audience that was once the college-age baby boom of the Sixties. Who is making pop music for it? Can rock in its purest form adapt itself with honor to a mass adult audience? And if not, how can the stylistic palette be diversified without losing the focus and intensity of the best music that has been created since the mid-Fifties? A retrogression to Tin Pan Alley idioms, big bands and studio orchestras is clearly not the answer to this dilemma, no matter what the stodgier WNEW nostalgists might wish or how many millions buy Linda Ronstadt's Riddle-arranged, Sinatra-inspired records. Nor can we expect Sinatra himself, despite the conviction and invention of *L.A. Is My Lady,* to lead us to a new stylistic synthesis.

But there are singers and songwriters, some of them rock and soft-rock veterans, others newcomers, still others cabaret artists from the gay culture of the Seventies, who are struggling to create that music. And at least now we may have begun to heal the angry scar of 1955, with once-bitter battlers on both sides beginning to recognize that there is great music and trashy music created in every style. Rock and Tin Pan Alley are the catchwords for the mainstream popular music of two different generations. They share many of the same roots, in European and American popular and even classical music. And they answer most of the same needs—our impulses to dance, to make love and to reach out emotionally. Popular music, with all its divisions and polemics, simply isn't so riven into antithetical factions as we may once have believed.

As rock composers and audiences grow older, too, we begin to realize how much our own generational struggles blinded us to our parents' values. "People seem grateful for this album in a way I've never experienced before," Ronstadt told the *New York Times*, speaking of the success of her 1983 *What's New*. "Older people finally feel included and validated in some way." What's refreshing about the Eighties climate of acceptance is that it represents not a betrayal of the music one has loved, but a welcoming of new musical experiences that enrich the familiar.

In all of this, Sinatra is not just one more musical artifact from the past that can be picked up and admired anew. He remains a vital contributor to the Tin Pan Alley tradition that nurtured him and that he, in turn, has done so much, for so long, to sustain. No one, not even the Who, spoke more truly for "his generation." And yet by now, after fifty years of professional singing, Sinatra can well claim to have transcended not just his own generation but his own country. He belongs to everyone now, and every nation. Even Australia.

"An American classic," Rosalind Russell once called him, and the phrase rings true. The *American* is clear enough, however universal he may now appear; there are those who argue that real universality can be attained only through

In Barbara, a former Las Vegas showgirl, Sinatra found the kind of glamorous yet supportive wife that had eluded him in his three previous efforts. Next page: Celebrating his sixty-fourth birthday in December 1979 at Caesar's Palace in Las Vegas. ASCAP would honor his forty-odd years in show business by presenting him with its first Pied Piper Award. On hand for the occasion were Paul Anka, Milton Berle, Glenn Ford, Rich Little, Harry James, Sammy Cahn, Dionne Warwick, Henry Mancini and Jule Styne.

Dancing with the First Lady at a White House celebration in February 1981, as President Ronald Reagan cuts in. By now Sinatra had become a political conservative, supporting Reagan's candidacy and presiding over his inaugural festivities. Like Reagan, he had come to believe that "the huge machine of central Government" was an oppressive force in American life.

For a benefit concert in March
1984 at Radio City Music Hall,
Sinatra joined the Motown
superstar, Diana Ross, and the
operatic tenor Luciano Pavarotti.

fidelity to one's deepest roots. But a *classic*? A classic is something timeless, something that has contributed to the evolution of culture in a way that mere singers, and popular singers at that, are not supposed to be able to do.

But if anyone, or anything, is a classic, it is Sinatra. His interpretations have shaped a half-century of song, transforming creativity into audible reality. He has validated an entire vernacular tradition and forced people to recognize its claims to classic status. Beyond all that, through his music and, yes, through his life, he has enriched the very idea of "classiness": not as something cold and marmoreal, free from human imperfection, but as a living, breathing, loving, hating human being. Art and life have sparred fitfully during this century, with some of the best art recoiling from the horrors of our time. Today we are beginning once again to recognize the place of human feeling in song, and no singer of our time has better invested the widest range of emotion in his music than Frank Sinatra.━

Artistic Chronology

The following year-by-year listing includes Sinatra's major electronically preserved artistic documents—his recordings and his films. The films exclude nonsinging cameo appearances. In order to avoid forgotten ephemera, the only singles included are those that made the *Billboard* magazine Top Ten chart. For albums, however, any release that appeared on the *Billboard* album chart is listed.

This chronology is meant to indicate the correlation of key Sinatra records and films at the time they were created and released. Since the original release dates, innumerable compilation albums have come out, and many albums have been rereleased, sometimes with different titles and configurations; none of these is included here. In addition, there is a burgeoning market of pirated Sinatra recordings, which are also not included.

Notable official Sinatra compilations include *Harry James's Greatest Hits* on Columbia; *The Tommy Dorsey/Frank Sinatra Sessions*, three two-disc albums, plus a single LP of *Radio Years*, including the first Axel Stordahl solo sessions from 1942, all on RCA; *The Frank Sinatra Story in Music*, *The Essential Frank Sinatra* and *Frank Sinatra, 1943 to 1951*, all on Columbia; *The Rare Sinatra* on English EMI, and *Sinatra*, Original Master Recordings' sixteen-disc boxed set of the key Capitol albums in audiophile pressings. In addition, Sinatra is said to be assembling a major retrospective package of his career for release in conjunction with his seventieth-birthday celebration in late 1985.

No albums are listed here before Sinatra's signing with Capitol Records in 1953. Columbia Records invented the LP and introduced it in 1948, but the Sinatra LPs that appeared on that label consisted almost exclusively of material that appeared originally or simultaneously on 78 rpm singles. It was only after he had joined Capitol and made his comeback, and after the LP had established itself commercially in the early Fifties, that Sinatra became primarily an album artist; thereafter, his Top Ten singles were relatively few.

1940

SINGLES (VICTOR, with Dorsey)
"I'll Never Smile Again"
"Imagination"
"Trade Winds"
"Our Love Affair"
"We Three"
"Stardust"

1941

SINGLES (VICTOR, with Dorsey)
"Oh, Look at Me Now"
"Do I Worry?"
"Dolores"
"Everything Happens to Me"
"Let's Get Away from It All"
"This Love of Mine"
"Two in Love"

FILM
Las Vegas Nights

1942

SINGLES (VICTOR, with Dorsey)
"Just as Though You Were Here"
"Take Me"
"Daybreak"
"There Are Such Things"

FILM
Ship Ahoy

1943

SINGLES
"It Started All Over Again" (VICTOR, with Dorsey)
"All or Nothing at All" (COLUMBIA, with James, recorded and first released in 1939)
"In the Blue of Evening" (VICTOR, with Dorsey)
"It's Always You" (VICTOR, with Dorsey)
"You'll Never Know" (COLUMBIA)
"Close to You" (COLUMBIA)
"Sunday, Monday or Always" (COLUMBIA)
"People Will Say We're in Love" (COLUMBIA)

FILMS
Reveille with Beverly
Higher and Higher

1944

SINGLES (COLUMBIA)
"I Couldn't Sleep a Wink Last Night"
"White Christmas" (rereleased in 1946 and also Top Ten)

FILM
Step Lively

1945

SINGLES (COLUMBIA)
   "I Dream of You"
   "Saturday Night"
   "Dream"
   "Nancy"

FILMS
   Anchors Aweigh
   The House I Live In

1946

SINGLES (COLUMBIA)
   "Oh! What It Seemed to Be"
   "Day by Day"
   "They Say It's Wonderful"
   "Five Minutes More"
   "The Coffee Song"

FILM
   Till the Clouds Roll By

1947

SINGLE
   "Mam'selle" (COLUMBIA)

FILM
   It Happened in Brooklyn

1948

FILMS
   The Miracle of the Bells
   The Kissing Bandit

1949

SINGLE
   "The Huckle Buck" (COLUMBIA)

FILMS
   Take Me Out to the Ball Game
   On the Town

1951

FILMS
   Double Dynamite
   Meet Danny Wilson

1953

FILM
   From Here to Eternity

1954

SINGLES (CAPITOL)
   "Young at Heart"
   "Three Coins in the Fountain"

LPs (CAPITOL)
   Songs for Young Lovers
   Swing Easy

FILM
   Suddenly

1955

SINGLES (CAPITOL)
   "Learnin' the Blues"
   "Love and Marriage"

LP
   In the Wee Small Hours (CAPITOL)

FILMS
   Young at Heart
   Not as a Stranger
   The Tender Trap
   Guys and Dolls
   The Man with the Golden Arm

1956

SINGLE
   "Hey, Jealous Lover" (CAPITOL)

LP
   Songs for Swingin' Lovers (CAPITOL)

FILMS
   Johnny Concho
   High Society

1957

LPs (CAPITOL)
   Close to You
   A Swingin' Affair
   Where Are You?
   A Jolly Christmas

FILMS
   The Pride and the Passion
   The Joker Is Wild
   Pal Joey

1958

LPs (CAPITOL)
   Come Fly with Me
   Only the Lonely

FILMS
   Kings Go Forth
   Some Came Running

1959

LPs (CAPITOL)
Come Dance with Me
Look to Your Heart
No One Cares

FILMS
A Hole in the Head
Never So Few

1960

LP
Nice 'n' Easy (CAPITOL)

FILMS
Can-Can
Ocean's Eleven

1961

LPs
Sinatra's Swingin' Session (CAPITOL)
All the Way (CAPITOL)
Ring-a-Ding-Ding (REPRISE)
Come Swing with Me (CAPITOL)
Sinatra Swings (REPRISE)
I Remember Tommy (REPRISE)

FILM
The Devil at Four O'Clock

1962

LPs
Sinatra and Strings (REPRISE)
Point of No Return (CAPITOL)
Sinatra Sings of Love and Things (CAPITOL)
Sinatra and Swingin' Brass (REPRISE)
All Alone (REPRISE)

FILMS
Sergeants Three
The Manchurian Candidate

1963

LPs (REPRISE)
Sinatra–Basie
The Concert Sinatra
Sinatra's Sinatra

FILM
Come Blow Your Horn

1964

LPs (REPRISE)
Days of Wine and Roses
Sinatra–Basie: It Might as Well Be Swing
Softly, As I Leave You

FILMS
Four for Texas
Robin and the Seven Hoods

1965

LPs (REPRISE)
Sinatra '65
September of My Years
A Man and His Music
My Kind of Broadway

FILMS
None But the Brave
Von Ryan's Express
Marriage on the Rocks

1966

SINGLES (REPRISE)
"Strangers in the Night"
"That's Life"

LPs (REPRISE)
Moonlight Sinatra
Strangers in the Night
Sinatra–Basie: Sinatra at the Sands
That's Life

FILM
Assault on a Queen

1967

SINGLE
"Somethin' Stupid" (REPRISE, with Nancy Sinatra)

LPs (REPRISE)
Francis Albert Sinatra & Antonio Carlos Jobim
Frank & Nancy

FILMS
The Naked Runner
Tony Rome

1968

LPs (REPRISE)
Francis A. & Edward K.
Cycles

FILMS
The Detective
Lady in Cement

1969

LPs (REPRISE)
My Way
A Man Alone

1970

LP
Watertown (REPRISE)

FILM
Dirty Dingus Magee

1971

LP
Sinatra & Company (REPRISE)

1973

LP
Ol' Blue Eyes Is Back (REPRISE)

1974

LPs (REPRISE)
Some Nice Things I've Missed
The Main Event/Live from Madison Square Garden

1977

TV FILM
Contract on Cherry Street

1980

LP
Trilogy (REPRISE, three discs)

FILM
The First Deadly Sin

1981

LP
She Shot Me Down (REPRISE)

1984

LP
L.A. Is My Lady (QWEST)

Books and Articles

DOUGLAS-HOME, ROBIN, *Sinatra* (New York: Grosset & Dunlap, 1962)

FRANK, ALAN, *Sinatra* (New York: Hamlyn, 1978)

GLEASON, RALPH J., "Frank: Then & Now," *Rolling Stone* 162, June 6, 1974

GODDARD, PETER, *Frank Sinatra: The Man, the Myth and The Music* (Don Mills, Canada: Greywood, 1973)

GOLDSTEIN, NORM, *Frank Sinatra: Ol' Blue Eyes* (New York: Holt, Rinehart & Winston, 1982)

HAMM, CHARLES, *Music in the New World* (New York: W. W. Norton & Company, 1983)

HAMM, CHARLES, *Yesterdays: Popular Song in America* (New York: W. W. Norton & Company, 1979)

HOWLETT, JOHN, *Frank Sinatra* (New York: Simon & Schuster/Wallaby Books, 1979)

KAHN, E. J., JR., *The Voice: The Story of an American Phenomenon* (New York: Harper and Brothers, 1947)

LEAR, MARTHA WEINMAN, "The Bobby Sox Have Wilted, But the Memory Remains Fresh," *New York Times* Arts and Leisure section, October 13, 1974

LONSTEIN, ALBERT I., *Sinatra: An Exhaustive Treatise* (New York: Musicprint Corporation, 1983)

LONSTEIN, ALBERT I., and MARINO, VITO R., *The Revised Compleat Sinatra*, with 1981 cumulative supplement (privately published, copyright 1970, 1979, 1981)

PETERS, RICHARD, *The Frank Sinatra Scrapbook* (New York: St. Martin's Press, 1982)

PLEASANTS, HENRY, *The Great American Popular Singers* (New York: Simon & Schuster, 1974)

RIDGWAY, JOHN, *The Sinatrafile*, three volumes (Birmingham, England: John Ridgway Books, 1977, 1978, 1980)

RINGGOLD, GENE, and McCARTY, CLIFFORD, *The Films of Frank Sinatra* (Secaucus, NJ: Citadel Press, 1971)

SCADUTO, ANTHONY, *Frank Sinatra* (London: Michael Joseph, 1976)

SHAW, ARNOLD, *Sinatra: The Entertainer* (New York: Delilah Books, 1982)

SHAW, ARNOLD, *Sinatra: Twentieth-Century Romantic* (New York: Holt, Rinehart & Winston, 1968)

SINATRA, FRANK, "Me and My Music," *Life*, April 23, 1965

SINATRA, FRANK, in collaboration with his voice teacher, John Quinlan, "Tips on Popular Singing" (New York: Embassy Music Corporation, 1941)

SINATRA, FRANK, "We Might Call This the Politics of Fantasy," *New York Times*, July 24, 1972

TALESE, GAY, "Frank Sinatra Has a Cold," *Esquire*, April 1966; reprinted in Talese's collection, *Fame and Obscurity* (New York: Dell, 1981)

WILSON, EARL, *Sinatra: An Unauthorized Biography* (New York: Macmillan, 1976)

Index

Page numbers in *italics* refer to captions.

Agnew, Judy, *216–217*
Agnew, Spiro, 202, *216–217*
Allen, Peter, 192
Andreotti, Guilio, *216–217*
Andrews Sisters, *50*
Anka, Paul, 21, *234–235*
Anslinger, Henry, 102
Arlen, Harold, 151, 152
Armstrong, Louis, 191
Astaire, Fred, 152
Autry, Gene, 102
Avalon, Frankie, 62
Aznavour, Charles, 211

Bacall, Lauren, 121, *155, 156–157*
Bain, Donald, 111, *126–127*
Ball, Lucille, *86–87*
Balliett, Whitney, 182, 191
Barnet, Charlie, 142
Barrett, Rona, 212
Baryshnikov, Mikhail, 22
Basie, Count, 142, 152, 182, *196–197*, 231
Beatles, 91, 192, 201
Beatty, Lady Adele, 121
Beck, Joe, 191, 201
Belafonte, Harry, 102
Bellini, Vincenzo, 62
Bennett, Tony, 62, 102, 141
Benson, George, 222
Berle, Milton, *176, 234–235*
Berlin, Irving, 42, 142
Berry, Chuck, 192
Bishop, Joey, 171
Blair, Janet, *86–87*
Bloch, Bert, 81
Bogart, Humphrey, 121, *155*, 171, 221
Bogdanovich, Peter, 22
Borzage, Edna, *80*
Bowes, Major, *16*, 22, 31, *37*
Brando, Marlon, 131, *138*
Brecker Brothers, 222
Brent, Earl, 152
Brown, Edmund, *176*
Bull, Ole, 82
Burke, Johnny, 151
Burnett, Carol, 22
Burton, Richard, 22
Byrd, Charlie, 182

Cagney, James, *219*
Cahn, Sammy, *108*, 142, 151, *176, 185, 234–235*
Carney, Harry, *93*
Caruso, Enrico, 51
Castro, Fidel, 172
Cavaliere, Felix, 62
Cavanaugh, Dave, 132, 142, 151, 161, 192
Charioteers, *64–65*, 111
Cheshire, Maxine, 212
Clooney, Rosemary, 102
Cohn, Harry, 121
Cole, Nat "King," *99, 176,* 191
Collins, Judy, 221
Como, Perry, 62, 81, *113,* 141, 192, 221
Cooper, Mrs. Gary, *155*
Coppola, Francis Ford, 72
Costa, Don, 191
Crawford, Joan, *109*
Crosby, Bing, 31, *33,* 51, 62, *63,* 71, 72, 82, 121, 141, 181
Crowther, Bosley, 131
Cugat, Xavier, 111
Curtis, Tony, *176*

Dagmar, 111, *126–127*
Damone, Vic, 62, 192
Darin, Bobby, 62
Davidson, Jo, *94*
Davis, Sammy, Jr., 92, 112, *123,* 171, *187, 188–189*
Day, Doris, 192
de Haven, Gloria, *53,* 92
Dennis, Matt, 152
Denver, John, 192, 201
Diamond, Neil, 201, 222
DiMucci, Dion, 62
Donizetti, Gaetano, 62
Dorsey, Tommy, *16, 18–19, 26–27, 28–29, 30, 35,* 41, 42, 62, 71–72, 81, *93,* 101, 121, 132, 182, 191, 231
Douglas-Home, Robin, 131
Dressen, Charlie, *69*
Dunaway, Faye, 222
Durante, Jimmy, *86–87, 106–107*

Eckstine, Billy, 191
Edison, Harry "Sweets," 142, 191
Ekberg, Anita, 121
Elizabeth II, Queen of England, *160*
Ellington, Duke, 182
Ellman, Ziggy, 62
Evans, George, *23*, 91–92, 101, 112
Exner, Judith Campbell, 172

Faith, Percy, 192
Falkenberg, Jinx, *86–87*
Farrow, Mia, *198, 199*, 201
Feather, Leonard, 191
Fischer, Carl, 151
Fisher, Eddie, 102, 112, 171
Fitzgerald, Ella, 141, 182, *200*, 224–225
Ford, Gerald, 202
Ford, Glenn, *234–235*
Ford, Tennessee Ernie, 102
Forte, Fabian, 62
Foster, Stephen, 41
Francis, Connie, 62

Garavanti, Dom (uncle), 62
Garavanti, Domenico (grandfather), 62
Garavanti, Rosa (grandmother), 31
Gardner, Ava, 102, 112, 121, *123, 124, 125*, 141
Garland, Judy, *60, 193*
Garrett, Betty, *118*
Gaudio, Bob, 201
Gershwin, George, 42, 81–82, 142
Getz, Stan, 182
Giancana, Sam "Momo," 172
Gibbs, Georgia, 102
Giddins, Gary, 21
Gilberto, Astrud, 182
Gilmore, Voyle, 142, 151, *163*
Gleason, Ralph J., 192, 211
Goodman, Benny, *30*, 41, 42, 82
Grayson, Kathryn, *106–107, 110*

Haggart, Bobby, 151
Haley, Bill, 102
Hamill, Pete, 131, 202
Hammerstein, Oscar, 61
Harrison, George, 201
Hart, Lorenz, 151
Hart, Moss, *84*
Haymes, Dick, 81
Hayworth, Rita, *154*
Heifetz, Jascha, 62, 71
Hirschfeld, Al, *95*
Hoboken Four, *16*, 31–32, 52
Hodges, Johnny, *93*
Holden, Stephen, 21, 132, 168–169, 191
Holiday, Billie, 71, 191, *224–225*
Holly, Buddy, 192
Holmes, Jake, 201
Hope, Bob, *63*
Hopper, Hedda, 102
Hughes, Howard, 102
Humperdinck, Engelbert, 141
Humphrey, Hubert, 202, *209*

Jackson, Michael, 222
James, Harry, *16, 18–19*, 32, 41, 61, 71, 72, 191, *234–235*
Jenkins, Gordon, 142, 151, *153*, 191
Jobim, Antonio Carlos, 182
Joel, Billy, 192
Jolson, Al, 51
Jones, Quincy, 152, *194–195*, 222, 231
Jourdan, Louis, *158*

Kael, Pauline, 131
Kahn, E. J., Jr., 71, 82, 92
Kaye, Danny, *160*
Kelley, Kitty, 212, 222
Kelly, Gene, *34*, 92, *114–115*, 122, *176*
Kelly, Grace, *149*
Kennedy, Jacqueline, *180*, 181
Kennedy, John F., 172, *173, 175, 176, 180*, 181, 202
Kennedy, Robert F., 181, 202
Kern, Jerome, 42, 231
Khrushchev, Nikita, *158*
Kilgallen, Dorothy, 102
King, Carole, 201
Kirsten, Dorothy, 61
Knight, Arthur, 131
Koch, Edward, *230*

Lahr, Bert, *35*
Laine, Frankie, 62, 102, 111, 151
Lanza, Mario, 62
La Rosa, Julius, 62
Lawford, Peter, 171, *176, 177,* 181, *187*
Lear, Martha Weinman, 91
Leigh, Carolyn, 132
Leigh, Janet, *176*
Lewis, Jerry Lee, 192
Lind, Jenny, 82
Liszt, Franz, 82
Little, Rich, *234–235*
Lodice, Don, *86–87*
Loren, Sophia, *156–157*
Luciano, Lucky, 101
Lupino, Ida, 152

McCambridge, Mercedes, *129*
McGovern, George, 202
McGuire Sisters, 102
McKuen, Rod, 201, *213*
MacLaine, Shirley, 131, *158*
Maltz, Albert, 181
Mancini, Henry, *234–235*
Manilow, Barry, 141, 201, 222
Mankiewicz, Joseph L., 131, *138*
Marcus, Greil, 102
Marsh, Dave, 211
Martin, Dean, 62, 171, *187,* 192, *193,* 223
Martino, Al, 62
Marx, Barbara Blakely, *219, 220,* 221, *233*
Marx, Zeppo, *219,* 221
Mastin, Will, 92
Mathis, Johnny, 192
Maxwell, Marilyn, *86–87,* 101
Maxwell, Robert, 151–152
May, Billy, 41, 142, *150,* 182, 231
Mercer, Johnny, 142, 151, 152, 191
Mercer, Mabel, 71, 224–225
Merman, Ethel, *84*
Merrill, Robert, 61
Miller, Bill, 142, 152, 161
Miller, Glenn, 42, 142
Miller, Mitch, 111–112, *120, 126–127*
Mitchell, Joni, 192, 201
Monroe, Marilyn, 121
Monroe, Vaughn, 102
Moore, Phil, 111
Mortimer, Lee, *97,* 101, 102

Nelson, Willie, 201
Newman, Randy, 201
Nixon, Pat, *216–217*
Nixon, Richard, 202, 211, *216–217,* 221
Novak, Kim, *154, 155*

O'Brien, Virginia, *35*
Oliver, Sy, *93,* 111, 182

Paderewski, Ignace Jan, 82
Parsons, Louella, 102
Pavarotti, Luciano, 212, *238–239*
Pegler, Westbrook, 101
Peterson, Oscar, 182
Pied Pipers, 71, 111, 231
Piscopo, Joe, 22
Pleasants, Henry, 51–52, 61, 71
Porter, Cole, 81, 142, *149,* 151, 191
Powell, Eleanor, *35*
Presley, Elvis, 91, 102, 122, 171, *190,* 192, 211, 231
Pretenders, 22
Prowse, Juliet, 172, *183, 184, 185*

Quinlan, John, 61

Ragland, Rags, *85*
Ray, Johnnie, 102
Reagan, Nancy, *236–237*
Reagan, Ronald, *159,* 202–211, 222, *236–237*
Reed, Rex, 212
Reynolds, Burt, 22
Reynolds, Debbie, *144–145,* 196
Rich, Jimmy, 32
Richards, Johnny, 132
Riddle, Nelson, 22, 41, 81, 132, 142, 151, 152, 161, 162, *163, 168–169,* 191, 232
Rizzo, Jilly, 162, *230*
Rodgers, Richard, 61, 142, 151
Ronstadt, Linda, 22, 201, 232
Roosevelt, Eleanor, *174*
Roosevelt, Franklin Delano, 82, *84, 85,* 92, 101, 181
Ross, Diana, 212, *238–239*
Ruark, Robert, 101–102
Rubinstein, Artur, *83*
Rush, Barbara, *159*
Russell, Rosalind, 232
Rydell, Bobby, 62
Ryder, Mitch, 62

Sachs, Manie, 111
Safire, William, 212
St. John, Jill, 172
Sedaka, Neil, 192
Sex Pistols, 21
Shaw, Arnold, 12–21, 81, 131, 181
Shor, Toots, *85*
Shore, Dinah, *143*
Sigman, Carl, 152
Simon, George T., 32, 111
Simon, Paul, 192, 201
Sinatra, Christina (daughter), 101, *116*
Sinatra, Franklin Wayne, Jr. (son), *78,* 82, *116,* 172, 231
Sinatra, Martin (father), *16,* 22, 208
Sinatra, Nancy (daughter), *54–55, 59,* 82, *116,* 201, *206, 210*
Sinatra, Nancy Barbato (wife), 41, *56, 59,* 102, *117*
Sinatra, Natalie "Dolly" (mother), *14–15, 17,* 22, 31, 121, *220,* 221
Skelton, Red, *35, 80*
Slatkin, Felix, 142, *185*
Smith, Gerald L. K., 101
Sondheim, Stephen, 221
Springsteen, Bruce, 32, 62, 222
Stafford, Jo, *28–29,* 71, 81, 101
Starr, Kay, 102
Stordahl, Axel, 41, 61, 72, 81, *104,* 112, 132, 142, 152, 191, 231
Styne, Jules, *108,* 142, 151, *234–235*
Sutherland, Joan 152
Syms, Sylvia, 111

Talese, Gay, 31, 162, 172, 181, 212
Taylor, James, 201
Tharp, Twyla, 22, 152, 222
Thomson, Virgil, 62
Tibbett, Lawrence, 51, *90*
Tizol, Juan, 182
Truman, Harry S., 101
Turner, Lana, 101, 102

Valentino, Rudolph, 82
Vallee, Rudy, 31, 51, *57*
Valli, Frankie, 62
Vanderbilt, Gloria, 121, *130*
Van Heusen, Jimmy, 142, 151, *176*
Vaughan, Sarah, 141, 182, *224–225*
Vicious, Sid, 21, 81, 201, 231

Wagner, Richard, 82
Warwick, Dionne, *234–235*
Waterman, Sanford, 202
Wayne, John, 122, 181
Weavers, 102
Webb, Jimmy, 192
Webster, Ben, 182
Weisman, Frederick R., 162
Welk, Lawrence, 192
Welles, Orson, 86–87
Who, 171, 232
Whorf, Richard, *108*
Wilder, Alec, 72, 81, 111
Williams, Esther, *114–115*
Wilson, Earl, 21, 61, 181
Wonder, Stevie, 192
Wynn, Steve, 171

Young, Lester, 191
Young, Victor, 231

Zion, Sidney, 192

ABOUT THE AUTHOR

John Rockwell grew up in San Francisco, graduated from Harvard College and received a PhD in cultural history from the University of California at Berkeley. After working as a classical music and dance critic for the *Oakland Tribune* and the *Los Angeles Times*, he began writing about music of all kinds for *The New York Times* in 1972. He has contributed to *Rolling Stone*, the *Rolling Stone Illustrated History of Rock & Roll* and *The Ballad of John and Yoko*, and is the author of *All American Music: Composition in the Late Twentieth Century*.

PHOTO CREDITS

Photo Editor Ilene Cherna